TRAILS WEST

Paper
Inspirations

Paper
Inspirations

Over 35 illustrated
papercrafting projects

Cheryl Owen

David & Charles

A David & Charles Book

First published in the UK in 2003

Distributed in North America
By F&W Publications, Inc.
4700 E. Galbraith Rd.
Cincinnati, OH 45236
1-800-289-0963

A catalogue record for this book is available from
the British Library.

ISBN 0 7153 1409 2 hardback
ISBN 0 7153 1410 6 paperback (USA only)

Executive editor   Cheryl Brown
Executive art editor   Ali Myer
Book designer   Lisa Forrester
Desk editor   Jennifer Proverbs
Production controller Ros Napper

Printed in the UK by Butler & Tanner Ltd
For David & Charles
Brunel House   Newton Abbot   Devon

Visit our website at www.davidandcharles.co.uk

David & Charles books are available from all good bookshops; alternatively you
can contact our Orderline on (0)1626 334555 or write to us at FREEPOST EX2 110,
David & Charles *Direct*, Newton Abbot, TQ12 4ZZ (no stamp required UK mainland).

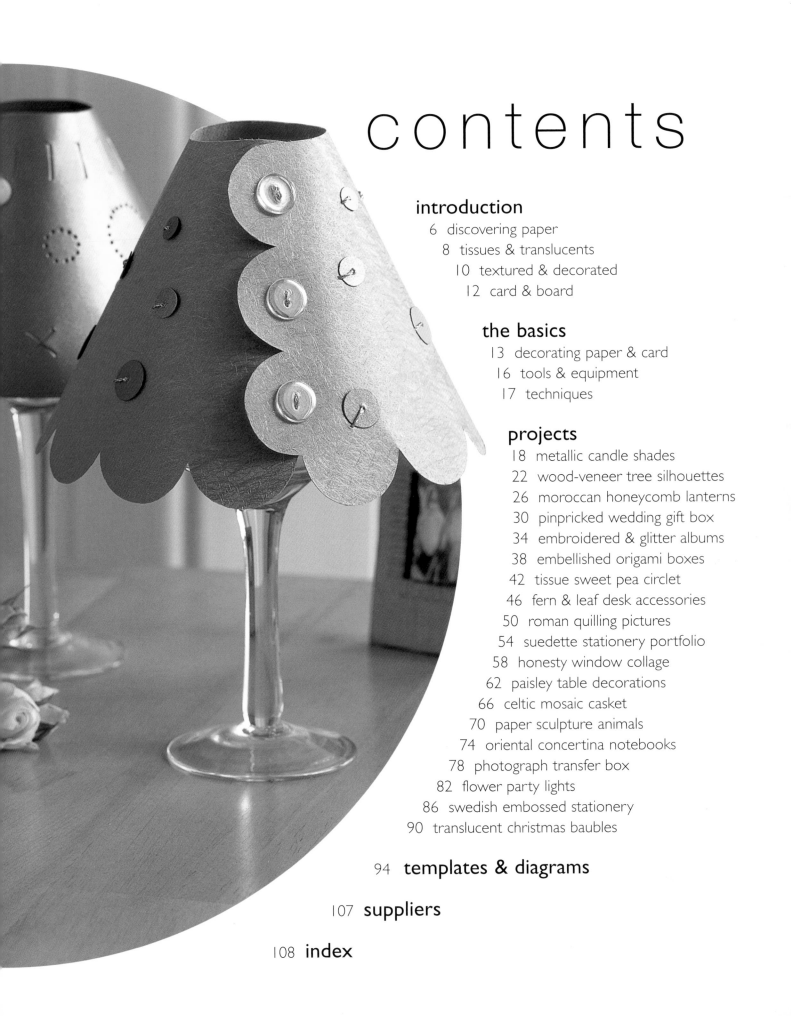

contents

introduction

the basics

projects

introduction

discovering paper

PAPER IS A SURPRISINGLY VERSATILE MEDIUM, readily available and easy to work with, but it is the fantastic array of enticing and exciting papers on offer today that really makes papercrafts so popular and such fun. This book presents masses of innovative ideas that incorporate all sorts of papers, from humble corrugated card to stunning handmade papers embedded with petals and foliage. Various techniques are demonstrated including traditional Japanese origami and paper quilling, as well as contemporary applications such as stamping and transfer methods. There are also lots of suggestions for creative ways to decorate plain paper and card, some using unexpected materials such as embroidery threads.

PART OF THE APPEAL OF PAPERCRAFTS is the accessibility of the tools and equipment needed, much of which you probably already own, even if you are a beginner. All the projects that follow would make wonderful gifts, although you may be tempted to keep them yourself! Clear step-by-step instructions accompany all the projects, and easy-to-use templates are provided to ensure a professional result. In addition, there is plenty of scope for creating your own designs, since an explanatory guide to the range of papers, with practical tips and suggestions for their use, is also included.

SO GO AHEAD TODAY AND DISCOVER the beauty and potential of paper – with so much to choose from, you will never tire of this endlessly creative material.

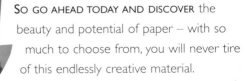

tissues & translucents

THE RANGE OF FINE TISSUES AND TRANSLUCENT PAPERS that is now available has extended an already exciting and varied choice of paper materials. These types of paper have generally been overlooked in the past, being thought to have limited use in paper crafts apart from functional tracing paper for making templates and tissue paper for flower-making and giftwrapping purposes. But even these humble examples have contemporary applications, as you can see in the three-dimensional Morrocan Honeycomb Lanterns on page 26, and the Tissue Sweet Pea Circlet on page 42. Images can be photocopied or scanned onto tracing paper which, when layered over different colours, takes on a completely different quality.

COLOURED TRACING PAPER, such as papers known as transparent satin or cromatico, are wonderful for collage work where layering the different colours creates new shades. Translucent papers such as scotia translucent and transmarque are faintly printed, while at the other extreme, brightly printed transparent papers are to be found in the giftwrap section of stores, often printed with bold, pop-art patterns.

VELLUMS are available from craft stores and by mail order, primarily for parchment craft. They are usually printed with subtle designs, some imitating lacework, and are often sold in small packs of coordinating designs. Traditionally prepared from animal skin, nowadays vellum is machine-made for general craftwork.

THAI PAPER is highly versatile and surprisingly robust. It incorporates delicate fibres that are distributed throughout the paper and is widely available in an attractive variety of colours.

JAPANESE HIKAKUSHI paper is also stronger than it looks and has an artless, spattered appearance.

JAPANESE ASARAKUSHI seems to have more holes than paper! It looks very effective layered over a contrasting colour. Some thin handmade papers have delicate designs of holes, which are created by spraying a fine jet of water onto freshly made sheets of paper.

tissue paper

Inexpensive tissue paper is far more versatile than you may think and can be successfully used to create three-dimensional effects and decorations.

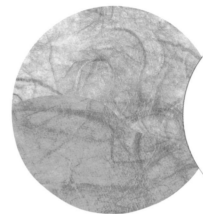

thai paper

This pretty paper is widely available in lots of colours from art and craft suppliers and some general stores, where it is sold for giftwrapping purposes.

technical tips

Tissues and translucent papers need extra attention when gluing as some adhesives will be visible on the right side. Spray adhesive is best for large areas, although it is difficult to achieve a smooth result on large pieces of tissue paper. Despite its lack of strength, paper glue is good for gluing small pieces, or use double-sided adhesive tape, bearing in mind that it may be noticeable from the right side on papers with holes. Remember to test any adhesive first on leftover paper. Do not cut soft fine papers such as tissue or Thai paper with a craft knife as it will tear the surface – use sharp scissors instead.

transparent satin

These smooth, evenly coloured papers come in different weights. They are very practical to use with templates as their see-through quality allows easy pattern tracing.

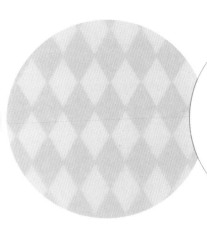

vellum

Mass-produced vellums are printed with subtle designs and come in plain colours. They are very popular for parchment craft.

printed transparent

These brightly printed papers are sold as giftwrap. Although transparent, their dense patterns make them quite opaque.

japanese asarakushi

Spray-mount this extraordinary paper onto a contrasting colour to show off its holey effect, or use it singly as a window hanging.

transmarque

The cloud-like appearance of this translucent paper makes it very versatile, and is ideal as a background paper for greetings cards.

japanese hikakushi

This finely textured paper comes in a limited range of subtle colours. For extra durability, spray-mount it onto a plain paper or card.

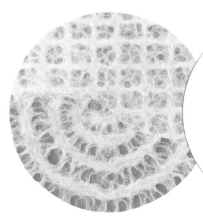

handmade paper

This includes paper with delicate designs of holes, such as lines and spirals. Use these delicate papers for creating collages and window hangings.

scotia translucent

This understated design of irregular printed white lines on a translucent paper works well with a coloured paper behind it.

textured & decorated

BEAUTIFUL TACTILE, TEXTURED AND PATTERNED PAPERS are the sort of papers that, being so irresistible, are often bought on impulse. Part of the attraction is the unique handcrafted quality of many of these papers, since no two are exactly the same. Some machine-made papers also have the look and feel of a handmade paper but are much cheaper to buy.

IF YOU MAKE YOUR OWN PAPER or enjoy experimenting with marbling paper, you will have the opportunity to use your own creative papers in most of the projects in the book. The Photograph Transfer Box on page 78 and the Flower Party Lights on page 82 display handcrafted papers to great effect.

ECHIZEN WASHI is a beautiful paper from Japan —'washi' means 'handmade paper' in Japanese. It is scattered with delicate, silky fibres and sometimes incorporates fragments of gold or silver. Although relatively expensive, it comes in large sheets. Echizen washi is used for one of the Metallic Candle Shades on page 18 and the Fern & Leaf Desk Accessories on page 46.

EMBOSSED PAPERS have raised or recessed images on the surface. This is achieved by forming the paper on or pressing it against a textured surface. The thicker the paper, the deeper the definition will be.

HANDMADE EMBEDDED PAPERS have all sorts of interesting materials incorporated into them, such as wafer-thin slivers of tree branches, leaves, petals or yarn.

SURFACE-DECORATED PAPERS are embellished once the paper has been formed. Paint, glitter or embroidery threads can be applied to paper – the latter kind is used in the Embroidered & Glitter Albums on page 34. For ideas on creating your own embellishments, see page 13. Marbled papers are created by swirling oil-based colours onto a water bath and placing a sheet of paper on top.

echizen washi

This elegant paper has many applications and is so attractive in its own right that little or no further decoration is required.

embossed paper

This tactile paper will lend a three-dimensional feel to a paper collage.

technical tips

The random patterning of many textured and surface-decorated papers makes their positioning crucially important, therefore experiment with placing the papers so that the embellishments and designs are shown at their best. Do not use embossed papers where their interesting surfaces could be squashed – for the pages of an album or framed behind glass, for example. Take care if cutting embroidered and embedded paper with a craft knife – the blade may catch the embellishments and rip them out. Replace the blade before cutting. Many handmade papers are quite thick and need a strong adhesive. Always test the glue on scraps of the paper. Art and hobby spray adhesive is stronger than spray mount adhesive. Use art and hobby spray adhesive when sticking large areas of thick, handmade paper.

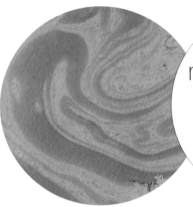

traditional marbled paper

Using marbled paper for a project immediately gives it a timeless, classical quality.

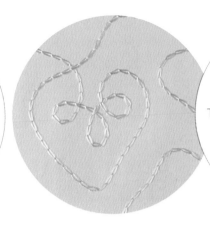

embroidered paper

This luxurious paper is available from specialist paper stores or suppliers. Neaten or cover the edges of embroidered paper, otherwise the embroidery may unravel.

gold marbled paper

The use of metallic paint in marbling makes it particularly majestic, and marbling on a soft, creased paper gives it the texture of a luxurious fabric.

fibrous paper

This richly textured paper is ideal for lots of paper crafts, from graphic three-dimensional flowers to collages. It is available from specialist art stores or suppliers.

woven-effect paper

Paper is pressed onto fabric with a distinctive weave to create a realistic woven-cloth surface. A collage of these papers incorporating embroidery stitches would be effective.

embedded-picture paper

This paper is a work of art in its own right. Pressed sprays of leaves are arranged on freshly made paper, then a fine layer of paper is couched on top to trap the foliage in place.

glitter-patterned paper

This machine-made paper adds a touch of glamour. Create your own glitter patterns with glitter relief paint or loose glitter (see pages 15 and 17).

embedded paper

Natural materials are incorporated at the paper-forming stage to create these beautiful papers. Handmade embedded papers are always expensive, but small sheets are often available.

card & board

PLAIN CARD AND BOARD forms the basis of many papercrafts, but there are also lots of decorative cards to choose from. These often have a slightly textured surface or a coloured coating.

STRAW BOARDS OR TICKET CARD are inexpensive, thick grey boards used to make sturdy items such as the letter rack on page 46 and the Suedette Stationery Portfolio on page 54. Mounting board can also be used for the same purposes but it is not a cheap option, so only use mounting board if you have offcuts to spare.

COLOURED CARD comes in different weights and colours, and is widely available from stationery and art stores or suppliers. See the Paisley Table Decorations on page 62 where coloured card has been highly decorated.

STENCIL SHEET is a thin oiled card used to make stencils. The oiled surface stops paint seeping through and makes it hard-wearing.

COATED CARD is white card coated with a shiny surface. It comes in many finishes including metallics, plain colours and iridescent effects. Textured metallic surfaces such as ridged and hammered metals are available. A pearlized metallic card has been used to frame the Honesty Window Collage, page 58.

TRE KONER is a thin card with a laid surface giving it a subtle ridged effect. It is widely available in lots of colours and makes an interesting background for making greetings cards.

technical tips

If you cannot find a card you like for a project, spray-mount a decorative paper onto thin card to use. The Photograph Transfer Box on page 78, for example, is made from a beautiful handmade paper applied to thin card. Use a craft knife, resting on a cutting mat, to cut card and board, since scissors will not be strong enough for thick card and board, and thin card will crease. To fold a coated card, either use a bone folder or score it on the wrong side with a craft knife so that the coated top surface remains unbroken, to prevent revealing the card backing.

coloured card
Coloured card is inexpensive and very versatile. Its thickness makes it quite robust and offers lots of scope for further decoration.

cromalux
This is a thin white card with a shiny coating. It comes in a multitude of colours and suits contemporary projects with clean lines.

tre koner
This thin textured card is often available in standard writing-paper size, making it ideal if just a small amount is required.

pearlized metallic card
The pearlized effect of this type of card is much more subtle than shiny metallic card.

corrugated card
This has an understated appeal and is available in various colours and thicknesses of corrugation.

stencil sheet
As well as making stencils for painting, use stencil sheet to make stencils to emboss through.

the basics

decorating paper & card

THERE ARE LOTS OF WAYS TO CREATE YOUR OWN DECORATIVE PAPER AND CARD. Many innovative ideas are included in the projects featuring stamping (page 74), pinpricking (page 30) and cutwork (page 18). Alternatively, experiment with the ornamental options outlined here.

embroidery

There are such a lot of luxurious embroidery threads available that it seems a shame to restrict their use to fabric. Embroider on paper or card at least 120gsm in weight and keep the designs simple for maximum impact.

Pierce a hole through the paper with a needle before embarking on each stitch. Embroider the paper, knotting the thread ends to start and finish.

relief paints

Relief paints are great fun to use. They come in a plastic bottle or tube and are applied via a fine nozzle. Relief paints harden to a pearlized or glitter finish.

Apply the relief paint at random, or lightly draw a design with a pencil and trace along the drawing with the relief paints. Set aside to dry.

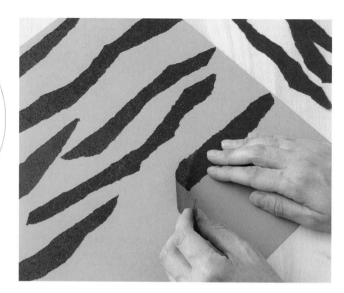

tissue paper découpage

Torn pieces of coloured tissue paper are very effective when applied to a contrasting coloured background.

Tear tissue paper into strips or squares. Stick to the background paper with spray mount adhesive.

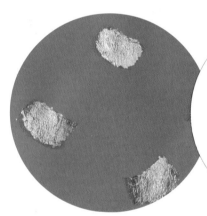

gold leaf

No other metallic effect has the brilliance and richness of gold leaf. Use transfer gold leaf in a simple, random pattern such as freehand stripes, dots or splodges.

1 Apply PVA (white) glue sparingly to the paper with a flat paintbrush.

2 Press a sheet of transfer gold leaf, metal side down, onto the glue.

3 Lift off the sheet. The gold leaf will have adhered to the glue.

4 Leave the glue to dry, then sweep away the excess metal with a soft brush.

stencilling

There are masses of ready-made stencils available for this popular craft but it is easy to cut your own from a stencil sheet.

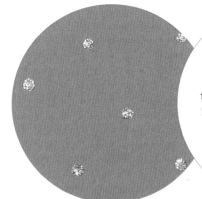

glitter

Loose glitter sparkles far more than relief-paint glitter. However, because of the way in which it is applied, it is suitable only for simple designs.

1 Cut the stencil from a stencil sheet with a craft knife, resting on a cutting mat.

1 Apply PVA (white) glue to the paper with a cocktail stick (toothpick).

2 Tape the stencil in place with masking tape. Apply acrylic paint to a ceramic tile or an old plate with a flat paintbrush. Dab at the paint with a stencil brush. Dab the paint through the stencil, holding the brush upright and moving it in a circular motion. Leave to dry, then remove the stencil.

2 Sprinkle the glitter on top, then shake off the excess onto another sheet of paper. Pour the glitter back into its container.

tools & equipment

For comfort and safety, work on a clean, flat, well-lit surface. Always keep sharp tools and glues beyond the reach of children and pets. Old plastic carrier bags cut open and laid flat will protect the surface underneath from glue and paint.

drawing

An HB pencil is best for drawing. Keep pencils sharpened to a fine point or use a propelling pencil. Always use a ruler and set square when drawing squares and rectangles so that the angles are accurate. Describe circles with compasses or use a circle stencil for small circles.

cutting

Sharp, pointed scissors are indispensable for paper crafts. Choose scissors that are comfortable to handle. Cut very intricate shapes with a small pair such as embroidery or manicure scissors. Craft knives give a neat cut and are better than scissors for cutting card. Cut with a craft knife on a cutting mat and replace the blades frequently, since a blunt blade will tear paper and card. Cut straight edges against a metal ruler. Pinking shears and deckle-edged scissors cut with a decorative edge and add a smart touch to many projects. Pierce holes with an awl or a bradawl. Use wire cutters or an old pair of scissors to cut wire and a small hacksaw to cut wood.

basic tool kit

Many of the following items are used in every project and are therefore not included in the materials and equipment lists. Gather these items together before you begin any project.

- sharp pencil
- scissors
- craft knife
- cutting mat
- metal ruler
- masking tape
- tracing paper
- scrap paper

sticking

Always read the manufacturer's instructions for adhesives and test them on scrap paper before use. PVA (white) glue is a versatile, non-toxic glue. It dries to a clear finish and will stick paper, card and wood. All-purpose household glue is also very useful for sticking small areas; it is not suitable for spreading over a large surface. Spray adhesives give an even coat of glue and are ideal for sticking large areas. Use spray mount adhesive to stick thin papers and card. Use art and hobby spray adhesive to stick thick paper, card and board. Double-sided adhesive tape provides a clean, neat way of joining layers together. Masking tape is very useful for sticking work temporarily in position. Use low-tack masking tape and check beforehand that it will not tear or mark the work.

Use a plastic spreader or an old paintbrush, or improvise with a scrap of card, to distribute glue evenly. Once you have designated an old brush to use for gluing, use it only for glue and clean it well after each application. A cocktail stick (toothpick) is useful for applying tiny amounts of glue.

painting & varnishing

Test paints on scrap paper before embarking on a painted paper project. Some paints may warp the paper. Acrylic paints are very versatile, the colours mix easily and the paint dries quickly. Use good-quality paintbrushes and clean them immediately after use. A natural sponge is very effective for applying paint in a random manner.

Polyurethane varnish is very hard-wearing and will protect découpaged items. Bear in mind that polyurethane varnish is oil based and will yellow the surface, whereas most water-based varnishes are clear although not usually so durable. Spray varnish will give gentle protection to projects. Do not use spray glues on items to be varnished, since the paper may wrinkle.

techniques

The same basic techniques appear in many of the projects. Several of the tools required will be in your basic tool kit (see facing page). Always read through the instructions for a project before embarking upon it and try out new techniques on spare scraps of paper first.

using templates

Trace the image onto tracing paper. Turn the tracing over and redraw it on the wrong side with a pencil. Use masking tape to tape the tracing right side up onto the surface. You may wish to transfer it to thin card to cut out and draw around, or transfer it directly onto the paper or card you want to use. Redraw the design to transfer it.

cutting

Straight edges on paper and card are best cut with a craft knife against a metal ruler, resting on a cutting mat. When cutting card or board, do not press too hard or attempt to cut right through at the first approach, but gradually cut deeper and deeper.

scoring

Scoring card will make it easier to fold. Thin card can be scored with a craft knife or a bone folder, which is a traditional bookbinder's tool. Score with the pointed end of a bone folder against a metal ruler. Take care not to cut right through the card – break the top surface only.

metallic candle shades

A variety of decorative effects have been applied to this trio of elegant shades for nightlight (tealight) holders. The shades are made from a range of highly realistic metallic card and papers. Accordingly, some of the methods of ornamentation involved are those that were traditionally used in metalworking.

To imitate the charming designs found in folk art metalware, a punched-tin technique is worked on copper-coloured card, while a delicate cutwork pattern is created using two sheets of differently coloured metallic paper applied together to make a single double-sided paper. Crosses and inverted 'V'-shapes are then cut into the outer surface and folded back to reveal the contrasting layer beneath. Circular card 'sequins' are sewn to a shade made from a paper called echizen washi, which is embellished with shiny copper-coloured fibres and has the appearance of a silky textile.

metallic candle shades

you will need

- 3 nightlight (tealight) holders with shades
- copper-coloured metallic card
- scrap paper or newspaper
- chisel
- hammer
- awl
- gold paper
- copper-coloured paper
- spray mount adhesive
- compasses or a coin
- brown paper impregnated with copper-coloured fibres (echizen washi)
- scrap of gold card
- crewel embroidery needle
- gold stranded embroidery thread
- 3 mother-of-pearl buttons
- 3 gold buttons
- 3 clear glass buttons

tip

If the paper for the sequin shade seems too flimsy to hold its shape well, apply two layers of paper together with spray mount adhesive.

1 Lay the original shade on a sheet of tracing paper to make a template. Lift one edge of the paper and tape it vertically to the shade with masking tape. Wrap the paper around the shade and tape in position. Draw along the upper and lower edges of the shade onto the tracing paper and mark where the paper meets the taped edge. Remove the template and add 1.5cm (⅝in) to the edge for the overlap. Make the lower edge deeper if you want a deeper shade than the original.

2 **To make the punched shade**, draw a row each of vertical lines, circles of alternating sizes and crosses 1.2cm (½in) inside the upper and lower edges of the template. Cut out the template. Tape the tracing onto a piece of copper-coloured card with masking tape and rest on layers of scrap paper or newspaper. Hold the chisel upright on one line. Hit the top of the handle with the hammer to punch the line. Continue on all the lines and crosses.

3 Hold the awl upright on a circle. Hit the top of the handle with the hammer to punch a hole. Move the awl around the circle to punch the outlines of the circles with holes spaced about 3mm (⅛in) apart. Draw around the outside of the template. Remove the template and cut out the shade.

4 **To make the cutwork shade**, draw a row of crosses 2cm (¾in) above the lower edge and two rows of inverted 'V's decreasing in size above the crosses on the template. Cut out the template. With wrong sides facing, apply gold paper to copper-coloured paper using spray mount adhesive. Tape the tracing to the gold side with masking tape. Resting on a cutting mat and using a craft knife against a metal ruler, cut along the lines through both layers.

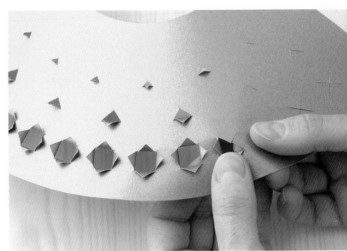

5 Draw around the outside of the template. Remove the template and cut out the shade. Carefully fold back the cutouts to reveal the copper-coloured layer beneath.

6 **To make the sequin shade**, draw scallops along the lower edge and one straight edge on the template. Cut out and use to cut a shade from the brown paper. Cut copper-coloured and gold card circles 1.2cm (½in), 1cm (⅜in) and 8mm (⁵⁄₁₆in) in diameter. Pierce a hole through the centres with a needle. Sew at random to the shade with gold stranded embroidery thread, bringing the needle up through the shade and the sequin hole, then inserting it back through the shade at the sequin edge. Fasten the thread on the underside.

7 To fasten the shades, overlap the straight edges by 1.5cm (⅝in). Sew three buttons in a row through both layers with gold stranded embroidery thread. Mother-of-pearl buttons were used on the punched shade, gold buttons on the cutwork shade and clear glass buttons on the sequin shade.

variation

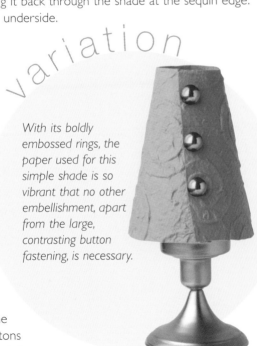

With its boldly embossed rings, the paper used for this simple shade is so vibrant that no other embellishment, apart from the large, contrasting button fastening, is necessary.

21

wood-
veneer tree
silhouettes

A selection of exciting and varied papers has been used to create these tree silhouettes. The choice of paper for the trees is a modern slant on the traditional art of cutting silhouettes, where a profile is cut from black paper and applied to a light-coloured background. Here, highly realistic wood-veneer paper has been used instead. Use the templates at the back of the book to re-create these tree designs, or draw your own, such as a favourite tree in your garden.

The silhouettes are applied to a cloud-effect paper and set on a translucent paper that has been subtly printed with a simple random design. The pictures are framed within a border of narrow strips of pine wood-veneer paper with interlaced corners, then mounted in inexpensive classic clip frames.

wood-veneer tree silhouettes

you will need

- mid-tone wood-veneer paper
- blue cloud-effect paper
- artist's paintbrush
- jar of water
- spray mount adhesive
- white printed translucent paper, e.g. scotia translucent paper
- sheet of standard-sized cream writing paper (A4 or US letter)
- pine wood-veneer paper
- 25 x 20cm (10 x 8in) clip frame

1 Trace a tree template on page 94 onto tracing paper using a pencil. Tape the tracing face down onto the wrong side of a piece of mid-tone wood-veneer paper with masking tape. Redraw to transfer the image. Using a craft knife and resting on a cutting mat, cut out the tree.

tip

Wood-veneer paper is available from specialist paper stores and suppliers and comes in a variety of wood finishes, such as pine, oak and silver birch.

2 To create the deckle edge to the cloud-effect paper, dip an artist's paintbrush in water and brush a line freehand on the paper to weaken it and render it easy to tear. Tear along the moistened line. Repeat to tear a rectangle approximately 19 x 14cm (7½ x 5⅝in). Carefully stick the tree centrally to the paper using spray mount adhesive.

3 To make the translucent paper opaque, stick it to a sheet of cream paper with spray mount adhesive. Cut a rectangle 25 × 20cm (10 × 8in) from the backed translucent paper using a craft knife against a metal ruler, resting on a cutting mat. Stick the torn cloud paper centrally to the translucent paper with spray mount adhesive.

4 Cut four 5mm (¼in) wide strips of pine wood-veneer paper 27cm (10¾in) long and four strips 22cm (8¾in) long. Spray the wrong side of the strips with spray mount adhesive. Place two long strips 5mm (¼in) apart 5mm (¼in) in from the long outer edges of the translucent paper with the ends extending beyond the edges of the paper. Repeat with the shorter strips on the short edges.

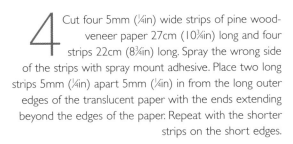

5 Press the strips in place at the centre. Working quickly before the adhesive dries, lift the ends of the strips at one corner and weave them under and over each other, starting with the inner strips. Smooth the strips outwards from the centre to stick them in place. Repeat on the remaining corners. Cut the ends level with the translucent paper. Finally, assemble the picture in the clip frame.

variation

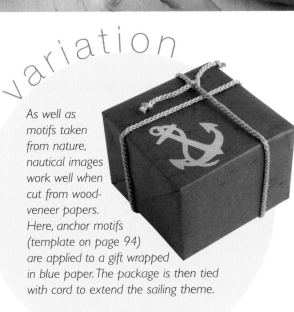

As well as motifs taken from nature, nautical images work well when cut from wood-veneer papers. Here, anchor motifs (template on page 94) are applied to a gift wrapped in blue paper. The package is then tied with cord to extend the sailing theme.

moroccan honeycomb lanterns

These jaunty lanterns are ingeniously created from layers of colourful tissue paper. A metallic cone 'hat' and silver beads give a radiant contrast to the delicate paper. A row of honeycomb lanterns would make a dynamic display suspended across a ceiling at a party.

The honeycomb technique of gluing layers of tissue paper shapes together is very easy and once mastered can be applied to your own designs. For instance, you can make contemporary versions of traditional honeycomb Christmas decorations and pop-out greeting cards. Experiment by layering contrasting coloured papers together, or use different delicate papers such as Thai paper. A crisp paper such as vellum won't work well – the choice of paper needs to be finely textured, lightweight and soft.

moroccan honeycomb lanterns

you will need

- blue tissue paper
- stapler
- 2 paperclips
- sewing thread
- crewel embroidery needle
- turquoise card
- spray mount adhesive
- 1 small silver bead
- silver thread
- silver drop bead with central hole
- paper glue
- double-sided adhesive tape
- silver card

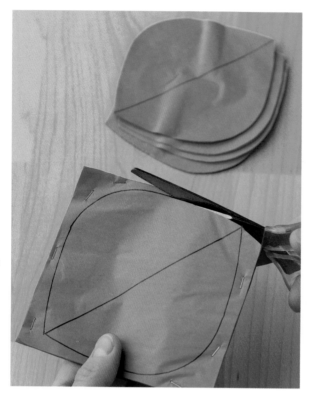

1 Place 24 layers of tissue paper, roughly 13cm (5in) square, in a pile. Trace the lantern template on page 95 onto tracing paper and use to draw the lantern on top, drawing along the solid outlines. Staple the layers together. Cut out the lantern. Repeat to cut out a total of 48 layers of lanterns.

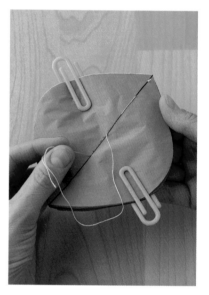

2 Stack the lanterns and secure with paperclips. Sew a running stitch through the layers along the centre line. Knot the thread at both ends

3 Use the lantern tracing to cut two lantern halves from turquoise card, cutting along the broken lines. Stick the halves, either side the central stitched line, to the top layer of tissue paper lanterns with spray mount adhesive.

tip

Be sure to use paper glue for the tissue paper – anything stronger may seep through to the underlying layers.

4 Thread a small silver bead onto a 90cm (1yd) length of silver thread. Thread both ends of the thread through the needle. Insert the needle up through a silver drop bead so that the beads hang in the centre.

5 Run a line of paper glue along the sewn line. Lay the silver thread along the glue so that the beads hang below the lantern and the threads extend above it for hanging.

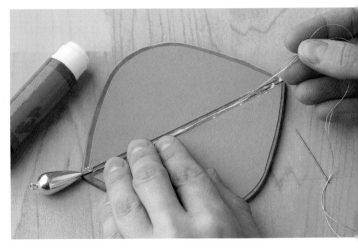

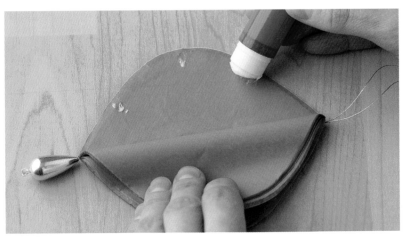

6 Place the lantern card side down. Lift all the halves on one side except the bottom one. Dab paper glue on the bottom half at the dots. Press down the next tissue half. Dab glue at the crosses, then press down the next tissue half. Continue to the top layer, alternating the application of glue at the dots and crosses.

7 Glue the other half in the same way, then fold in half to carefully stick the top halves together. Stick the card halves together with pieces of double-sided adhesive tape.

variation

Make an oriental lantern (template on page 95) from vibrant red tissue paper finished with a golden cone and shiny tassel. Red represents joy and celebration in China, where a colourful Lantern Festival is held in the first month of the Chinese New Year.

8 Use the template on page 95 to cut a cone from silver card. Pull the cone between your fingers to curve the card. Apply double-sided adhesive tape to the tab on the right side. Lap the straight edge over the tab and stick in place to form a cone. Dab paper glue inside the cone. Insert the needle up through the point of the cone and rest the cone on top of the lantern. Slip off the needle and knot the thread ends together.

pinpricked wedding gift box

The ultra simple technique of pricking a design on thin card is used here to sophisticated effect in creating an understated gift box – ideal for presenting a wedding gift.

The heralding cherub motif makes the design suitable for other special occasions too – perhaps to welcome a newborn baby or to celebrate an anniversary. A coordinating gift enclosure adorned with a pair of wings adds a whimsical touch.

This box is suitable for packaging any lightweight gift. Wrap it in sumptuous handmade tissue paper, maybe with a scattering of confetti as an extra surprise for the recipients. If you want to present a more weighty gift, paint a thick card or wooden box and pinprick the design on a square of thin card to glue to the lid.

pinpricked wedding gift box

you will need

- white card
- 10 sheets of kitchen towel
- compasses
- bone folder (optional)
- double-sided adhesive tape

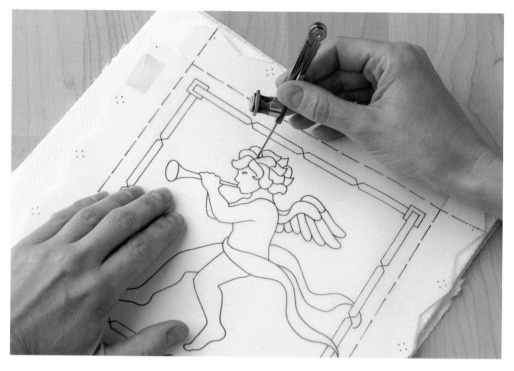

1 **To make the gift box**, enlarge the lid template on page 96, trace onto tracing paper and use as a template to cut a lid from white card with a craft knife, resting on a cutting mat. Tape the tracing to the card with masking tape. Rest the lid on the ten sheets of kitchen towel. Pinprick along the solid lines about 3mm (⅛in) apart and at the dots with the point of the compasses.

tip

The point of compasses will do the job of pinpricking efficiently, although specialist tools are available from craft stores and by mail order.

2 Remove the tracing. On the right side, score along the broken lines with a bone folder or craft knife against a metal ruler. Fold the lid backwards along the scored lines to form the lid shape.

3 Apply double-sided adhesive tape to the lid tabs on the right side. Peel off the backing tapes and stick under the opposite ends of the lid sides.

4 Refer to the diagram on page 97 to cut two box sides from white card. On the right side, score along the broken lines with a bone folder or craft knife against a metal ruler. Fold backwards along the scored lines. Apply double-sided adhesive tape to the end tabs on the right side and the base tabs on the wrong side. Peel the backing tapes off one end tab and stick under the straight end of the other box side.

5 Cut a 17.7cm (6⁵⁄₁₆in) square of white card for the base. Peel the backing tapes off the remaining tabs and stick the base tabs under the base. Stick the end tab under the opposite end of the box side.

6 To make the gift enclosure, cut a rectangle of white card 15 x 6cm (6 x 2¼in). On the right side, score down the centre, parallel with the short edges, with a bone folder or craft knife against a metal ruler. Fold in half along the scored line, then open out flat again. Trace the gift enclosure template on page 97. Tape the tracing to the front of the enclosure with masking tape. Rest the enclosure on the sheets of kitchen towel. Pinprick along the solid lines with the point of the compasses. Remove the tracing and refold the card.

variation

These pretty greetings cards have pinpricked wedding motifs (see page 97) worked on squares of laid paper cut with pinking shears. The pinked edges are highlighted with a border of pinpricks. The squares are then tied to folded rectangles of cloud-effect card.

embroidered & glitter albums

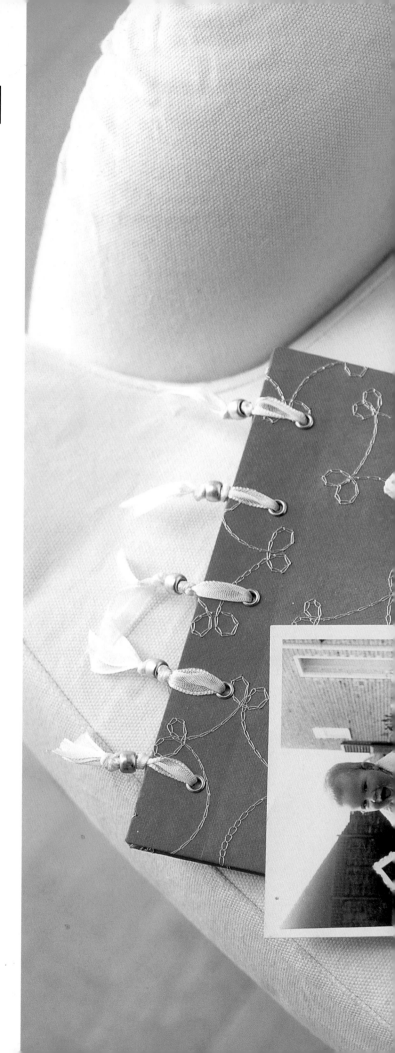

Luxurious papers with swirling patterns worked in embroidery and glitter cover these stylish albums. The papers are so beautiful in themselves that no further decoration is necessary, apart from ribbon fastenings to secure the pages. Standard-sized writing paper is used for the pages in contrasting colours.

Alternatively, you could decorate your own papers for the covers. Hand embroidery stitches using a few strands of metallic thread or even worked on a sewing machine would look superb. The size of paper needed is small enough to go through a sewing machine without creasing. Similarly, a design worked in dots applied with a glitter relief pen would be very attractive and quick to achieve.

embroidered & glitter albums

you will need

- thick card, e.g. 300gsm in weight
- bone folder
- embroidered or glittery paper
- PVA (white) glue
- 15 standard-sized sheets of coloured writing paper (A4 or US letter)
- sheet of scrap paper
- spray mount adhesive
- awl
- 10 metal eyelets
- eyelet fixing tool
- 1.5m (1²⁄₃yd) of 1.2cm (½in) wide white silk ribbon or pink organza ribbon
- large-eyed needle
- 5 silver pony beads, for white silk ribbon fastening

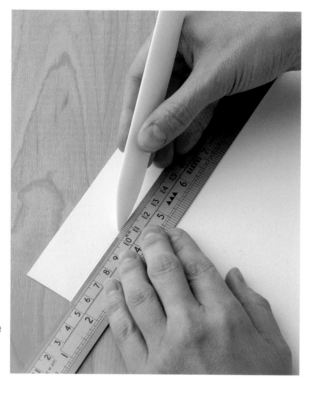

1 Cut two rectangles of card 30.5 x 22cm (12 x 8¾in) for the covers. Score across the covers 3cm (1¼in) from one short edge with a bone folder to form the hinge. Fold along the scored line, then lay the covers flat.

tip

Create your own embroidered covers by stitching random patterns on the covers with a sewing machine using metallic machine embroidery threads.

2 Cut two rectangles of embroidered or glittery paper measuring 33.5 x 25cm (13¼ x 10in). Place the covers centrally scored side down on the wrong side of the embroidered or glittery paper rectangles. Glue the corners, then the edges of the paper over the covers with PVA (white) glue.

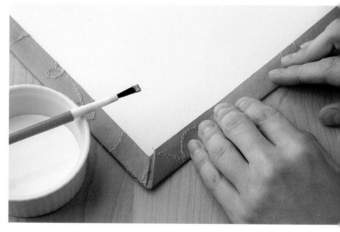

3 To line the covers, stick a sheet of the coloured writing paper centrally to the wrong side of the covers with the spray mount adhesive. Lay the remaining coloured paper sheets centrally on the back cover. Lay the front cover on top, matching the hinged edges.

4 Use the template on page 98 (either the A4 or the slightly shorter US letter version, depending on the paper you are using) to cut a hole guide from paper. Place the guide along the hinged edge. Resting on a cutting mat, pierce a hole through all the layers at each dot with the awl. Make the holes large enough to accommodate the eyelets.

5 Fix an eyelet through each hole of the covers with the fixing tool.

6 Layer the pages between the covers, matching the holes. Thread a 30cm (12in) length of white silk ribbon through each hole with a large-eyed needle. Tie the ribbons in a knot to secure the pages. Insert the ribbon ends through a pony bead. Knot the ribbons and cut the ends diagonally.

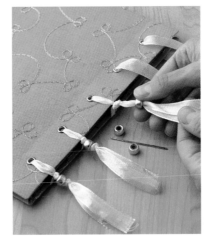

Variation

This pair of pretty bookmarks is cut from card and covered with embroidered paper. A beaded trim and tassel are glued to the lower edges, and then a piece of plain paper is applied to the underside with PVA (white) glue to cover the raw edges.

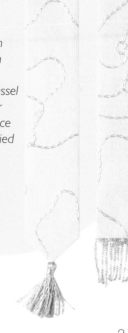

7 Alternatively, lace organza ribbon in and out of the holes, starting at the top on the front cover. Tie the ribbon ends together in a bow. Cut the ends in chevrons.

embellished origami boxes

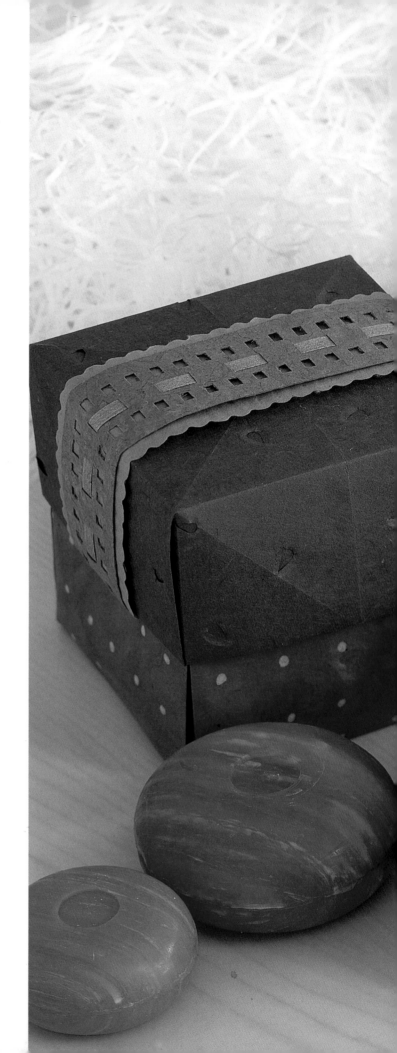

The Japanese art of origami is one of the most ancient and traditional of the paper crafts, and making origami boxes employs some of its simpler paper-folding techniques. Although usually worked in colourful origami papers, this set of smart boxes is constructed from plain and subtly printed and textured papers, including a pretty example with small teardrop shapes punched at random.

Use deckle-edged scissors, holepunches and a corrugator to trim your creations with bands of coordinating papers to add a further twist to this classic craft.

The boxes can be made from squares of paper of any size. The finished size of the box will be a third of the size of the paper. For example, a 30cm (12in) square of paper will make a square box 10cm (4in) tall by 10cm (4in) wide.

embellished origami boxes

you will need

- selection of plain, printed and textured papers
- deckle-edged scissors
- holepunches
- paper ribbon
- corrugator
- double-sided adhesive tape
- spray mount adhesive

1 Cut two squares of paper for the box and lid, cutting the square for the box with deckle-edged scissors. Refer to the diagrams on page 98 to fold the squares along the solid and broken lines with the wrong sides facing. Open the squares out flat again.

To make the box, refold the box square diagonally in half. Fold the corners at the end of the diagonal fold inwards along the broken lines.

2 Stand the corners upright along the broken lines, then fold them flat, matching the diagonal fold line to the broken lines. Crease along the new folds. Open the paper out flat. Repeat steps 1 and 2 on the other diagonal fold.

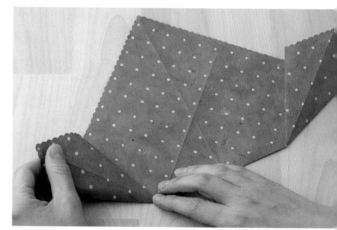

tip

A corrugator is a clever gadget through which strips of paper are fed, a handle is turned and the emerging paper strip is delicately corrugated.

3 With the wrong side of the paper facing upwards, fold along two adjacent base lines to form two sides of the box. Butt the broken lines together, folding the excess paper at the corners inside. Fold the triangle at the top of the box corner over the corner to hold the corner in place.

4 Recrease along the corner fold to define it. Repeat for the other corners to form the box.

5 **To make the lid**, lay the paper with the wrong side facing upwards. Fold two opposite corners of the lid square to the centre. Fold again so that the broken lines meet at the centre.

6 Lift the edges along the last pair of folds to form the sides of the lid. Lift and fold the third side of the box by bringing the third broken line level with the upright sides, folding the excess paper inwards at the corners. Repeat with the fourth broken line on the fourth side. Fold down along the broken lines so that the points meet at the centre, on the underside of the lid.

7 To decorate the lid, cut two or three strips of coordinating papers of different widths. (For example, cut 37cm (14¾in) lengths for a 10cm (4in) box.) Cut one of the strips with deckle-edged scissors. Embellish the strips by cutting a fringe along the edges, punching holes, cutting slits to slot with paper ribbon or by threading a strip through a corrugator.

variation

8 Lay the strips across the top of the lid, tuck the ends inside the lid and stick the ends in place with double-sided adhesive tape. To neaten, cut a square of paper 5mm (¼in) smaller on all sides than the lid. Stick the square inside the lid with spray mount adhesive, covering the ends of the strips.

Bands of paper give a coordinated look to giftwrapped presents. These packages are covered with leftover wallpaper and trimmed with strips of wallpaper, some cut with pinking shears and some cut along the outline of the embossed pattern. A corrugator adds a tactile dimension to some of the strips. A holepunched edging allows the underlying paper to show through. The matching gift tag completes the effect.

tissue sweet pea circlet

Petal shapes cut from inexpensive coloured tissue paper take on the delicate, crinkly characteristics of sweet pea petals if moistened and left to dry. The petals can then be assembled to create sprays of highly realistic blooms, complete with the trailing tendrils so typical of sweet peas.

The flowers are attached to wire stems, and therefore can be bent and draped to any shape. Here, twelve flower sprays are twisted together to make a garland, which is then formed into a classic ring of flowers. Create sprays in coordinating hues of tissue paper or choose one shade throughout for impact.

Sweet pea garlands and circlets, or just a simple posy tied with ribbon, make lovely decorations for a special occasion, such as a wedding feast or an important birthday. And of course, they won't wilt or need watering!

tissue sweet pea circlet

you will need

- coloured tissue papers
- sheet of plastic, e.g. cut from a plastic carrier bag
- artist's paintbrush
- jar of water
- cotton wool
- PVA (white) glue
- 0.05mm diameter wire
- wire cutters or an old pair of scissors
- cocktail stick (toothpick)
- green cartridge paper
- green floral tape
- 1mm diameter wire

1 For each sweet pea spray, use the templates on page 95 to cut four hearts, three small petals and four large petals from tissue paper. Lay the pieces on a sheet of plastic – if using a printed plastic carrier bag, use the unprinted side, in case the print stains the tissue. Use an artist's paintbrush to moisten the pieces. Leave to dry.

2 Roll four small balls of cotton wool, approximately 8mm (⅓in) in diameter. Squeeze to an oval. Glue each oval to the end of a 9cm (3½in) length of 0.05mm wire. Fold a heart around each oval, holding the point against the wire. Use a cocktail stick to apply a thin line of PVA (white) glue along the curved edge on one half of the heart. Press the curved edges together, enclosing the cotton wool. Set one wired heart aside for a 'bud'.

tip

Green floral tape, also known as gutta percha, is a strong, flexible tape that is impregnated with a waxy substance, which makes it self-adhesive. It is available from florists.

3 To make three florets for each spray, use the cocktail stick to run a thin line of glue along the centre of each small petal. Stick to the back of the remaining hearts, matching the lower points. Run a thin line of glue along the centre of two florets and stick two large petals to the back of each, matching the points. Leave to dry. Gently pull the petals backwards to open out the florets.

4 Use the template on page 95 to cut four calyxes and two leaves from green cartridge paper. Glue the lower point of each calyx around the bud and florets, matching the lower points. Bend the calyx tips outwards.

5 Snip two 7cm (2¾in) lengths of 0.05mm wire for the leaf stems. Cut the floral tape lengthways in half to make narrow strips. Bind diagonally around the stems, rolling the wire into the tape and stretching the tape as you work. Trim the excess. Glue each leaf stem to a leaf.

6 Snip a 20cm (8in) length of 0.05mm wire for the tendril. Bind with a narrow strip of floral tape. Bind the covered wire around a pencil to coil it. Slip the tendril off the pencil. Cut the end of a narrow length of floral tape diagonally. Bind around the bud and floret stems with the diagonal end against the calyxes, gluing in place to start. Trim the excess.

variation

Single sprays of sweet peas make impressive trimmings at a celebratory dinner. Wind a ruby coloured spray around the stem of a wine glass and napkin. After the event, they can be unwound and kept as keepsakes by your guests.

7 Hold the lower 2.5cm (1in) of the bud stem against the end of a 15cm (6in) length of 1mm wire for the spray stem. Bind the wires together with a narrow length of floral tape. Add the small floret, large florets, pair of leaves and tendril as you bind down the spray stem. Trim the excess tape and splay open the florets, leaves and tendril. Lay the sprays, overlapping, in a line. Twist the stems together to make a garland. Bend into a circle and twist the end of the last spray around the stem of the first (refer to the photograph on pages 42–43).

fern & leaf desk accessories

This handsome set of coordinating desk accessories will inspire even the most reluctant to tackle those routine administrative tasks. The sturdy letter rack will aid the filing of correspondence, and a glass paperweight is always useful for anchoring flyaway papers. The paperweight, available from craft stores and suppliers, has a recess underneath to which decorated papers can be applied. To complete the set, a traditional ink blotter features triangular corners for holding blotting paper firmly in place.

The woodland motifs are complemented by the papers used to make this smart stationery trio. The white decorative background paper is echizen washi paper, which incorporates fine, wispy fibres, while the ferns and leaf spray are cut from a fibrous paper. Various options here include papers containing banana leaves or onion skins. The finished letter rack is sprayed with matt varnish for protection.

fern & leaf desk accessories

you will need

- straw board
- white decorative paper, e.g. echizen washi
- PVA (white) glue
- glue brush, plastic spreader or scrap of card, for applying glue
- green fibrous paper
- 3cm (1¼in) wide x 1cm (³⁄₈in) thick wood
- hacksaw
- spray matt varnish
- hand- or machine-made paper embedded with petals and foliage
- round or oval glass paperweight
- light and dark green mulberry paper
- spray mount adhesive
- transparent sticky-backed plastic
- rectangles of blotting paper, 31.5 x 22cm (12½ x 8¾in)

tip

To prevent the straw board for the letter rack and blotter corners showing through the covering papers, you may need to paint the board with white acrylic paint, using a flat paintbrush.

1 **To make the letter rack**, use the template on page 99 to cut a front and back letter rack from straw board using a craft knife against a metal ruler on a cutting mat. Cut white decorative paper 1.5cm (⅝in) larger on all sides. Glue the front and back centrally on the wrong side of the paper with PVA (white) glue. Glue the corners, then the edges over the boards. Cut white decorative paper 5mm (¼in) smaller on all sides. Glue centrally to the front and back undersides.

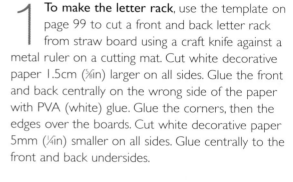

2 Carefully glue two 17 x 8cm (6¾ x 3¼in) rectangles of green fibrous paper together. Use the template on page 99 to cut out a fern frond with a craft knife, resting on a cutting mat. Apply glue to the wrong side and stick to the front.

3 Saw a 23cm (9in) length of wood. Glue green fibrous paper 28 x 8cm (11 x 3¼in) to it with PVA (white glue), sticking the edges to the underside.

4 Glue straw board 26 x 7cm (10¼ x 2¾in) for the base centrally to the wrong side of a 29 x 10cm (11½ x 4in) rectangle of green fibrous paper. Glue the corners, then the edges over the base. Glue green fibrous paper 25 x 6cm (9⅞ x 2⅜in) centrally to the underside. Glue the wood centrally on the base.

5 With right sides facing forwards, glue the back upright to the back long edge of the wood and the front upright to the front long edge. Allow to dry. Spray with varnish.

6 To make the paperweight, cut out a circle or oval from the petals and foliage paper to fit the paperweight recess. Use spray mount adhesive to apply two layers of mulberry paper together. Cut a fern tip or leaf spray from mulberry paper using the template on page 99. Stick to the circle or oval with spray mount. Draw around the paperweight on the backing of sticky-backed plastic. Cut out. Lay the circle or oval in the recess. Stick the plastic circle or oval to the paperweight underside.

7 To make the blotter, cut straw board 35.5 × 27cm (14 × 10½in) and white decorative paper 38.5 × 30cm (15¼ × 11¾in). Place the board centrally on the wrong side of the paper. Glue the corners, then the edges over the boards. Use the template on page 101 to cut four triangles from straw board, cutting along the broken and diagonal lines. Cut four 16 × 8.5cm (6¼ × 3⅜in) rectangles of green fibrous paper. With right sides down, place each triangle centrally on a rectangle, with the long edges of the triangle and rectangle parallel. Fold one long edge over the triangle. Glue in place.

variation

For this autumnal-hued holder for a 10cm (4in) jotter pad, use the diagram on page 102 to cut the holder side from thin card and cut a 10.3cm (4⅛in) square for the base. Make the holder referring to step 7 on page 65. Cover with black decorative paper. Glue a fern tip cut from orange fibrous paper to each side with PVA (white) glue.

8 Place one triangle right side up on the blotter. Slip the blotting papers under it. Hold the layers together and turn wrong side up. Glue the long edge of the green paper to the wrong side for 1.5cm (⅝in), catching in the blotter corner. Repeat at each corner. Glue a 35 × 26.5cm (13¾ × 10½in) rectangle of white decorative paper to the underside.

roman quilling pictures

The quills of porcupines and birds were originally used to make quilled pictures, hence the term for this traditional paper craft. Nowadays, the technique features coiled paper strips. The coils are gently squeezed into a variety of shapes to create a design. Sets of narrow strips of coloured papers are available from craft stores and by mail order specifically for quilling, although it is easy to cut your own strips in your chosen hues. Use 90–120gsm paper for the best results, and if using more than one colour, use the same weight of paper throughout.

These bold designs are inspired by Roman antiquities – a majestic column and an elegant amphora. The motifs are bordered with quilled squares that represent Roman mosaics and are set within painted picture frames that have been randomly sponged with black paint.

roman quilling pictures

you will need

- 16 x 11cm (6½ x 4½in) wooden picture frame
- fine glasspaper
- yellow or green acrylic paint
- 2cm (¾in) flat paintbrush
- black acrylic paint
- ceramic tile or an old plate
- natural sponge
- white card
- blue or yellow paper, 90–120gsm in weight
- black paper, 90–120gsm in weight
- cocktail sticks (toothpicks)
- PVA (white) glue

tip

Spray the design with clear spray varnish for protection. Alternatively, use a box frame so that the picture will then be sealed behind glass.

1 **To prepare the frame,** take it apart and discard the glass safely. Lightly sand the frame with glasspaper, then paint yellow or green using a flat paintbrush. Leave to dry. Apply a thin coat of black paint to a ceramic tile or old plate with a flat paintbrush. Dab at the paint with a moistened sponge. Dab the paint randomly onto the frame. Leave to dry. Cut a rectangle of white card to fit the frame.

2 Cut 4mm (³⁄₁₆in) wide strips of blue or yellow and black paper 20cm (8in) long with a craft knife against a metal ruler, resting on a cutting mat.
   To make the mosaics, roll the blue or yellow strips tightly around a cocktail stick – about 26 for one picture.

3 Release the coils so that they spring open. Use a cocktail stick to apply glue to one end. Stick the end against one side, forming a circle. Squeeze the circles in half, then pinch each half to form a square. Arrange on the card 2cm (¾in) inside the outer edges. Spread glue on the underside of the mosaics sparingly with a cocktail stick, then gently stick in place.

4 **To make the pediments,** fold under 4cm (1½in) at each end of two black strips. Lightly mark the midway point of the strips with a pencil. With the strip folded, coil each end around a cocktail stick for 4cm (1½in), with the short end against the stick. Release the coils. Butt the ends together and glue them to the midway point.

5 Coil six black strips around a cocktail stick. Release the coils slightly to loosen the grip on the stick. Glue the ends to one side to form a tight circle. Arrange the pediments on the picture with three tight circles along the inner edges. Glue in place.

6 Make nine black circles following steps 2 and 3. Squeeze in half. Pinch each half 5mm (¼in) from the first folds to form a rectangle. Glue in three rows of three between the pediments.

7 **To make the amphora handles,** lightly mark two black strips 5cm (2in) and 11.5cm (4½in) from one end. Fold under the end at the 5cm (2in) mark. Coil the folded end around a cocktail stick for 5cm (2in), with the short end against the stick. Release the coils. Glue the coiled end to the 11.5cm (4½in) mark. Coil the other end around the stick in the opposite direction for 5cm (2in).

8 **To make the double coil decorations,** mark the midway point of three black strips with a pencil. Coil each end as far as the midway point around the cocktail stick. Release the coils. Coil six black strips. Release the coils slightly to loosen the grip. Glue the ends to one side to form a tight circle. Make three black circles following steps 2 and 3. Arrange the amphora pieces between the handles. Glue in place. Once completely dry, carefully place the finished picture in the frame and secure.

variation

Stick eight colourful quilled squares in grid formation to the front of a greetings card. Place a piece of bubble-wrap over the card to protect it if sending it by mail.

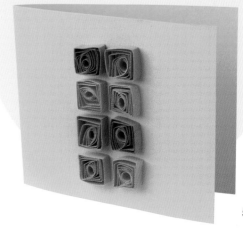

suedette stationery portfolio

Plush suede-effect paper in a regal shade of purple covers this distinguished-looking portfolio. Contrast is achieved with cream leatherette paper on the hinge, traditionally reinforced corners and a pair of gusseted pockets, which can safely store stationery, artwork or photographs. A lining of delicately speckled cream paper adds a further contrast and sophistication.

The portfolio fastens with grosgrain ribbon and has an understated label bordered with a scallop-edged surround cut with deckle-edged scissors. The label is stamped with a row of silver feathers recalling elegant writing quills from a bygone era. Rubber stamps with a variety of motifs are available from craft and stationery stores.

suedette stationery portfolio

you will need

- straw board
- cream leatherette paper
- PVA (white) glue
- glue brush, plastic spreader or scrap of card, for applying glue
- purple suede pile flock paper
- 70cm (28in) of 2.5cm (1in) wide cream grosgrain ribbon
- cream speckled paper
- bone folder (optional)
- 1.5cm (⅝in) wide double-sided adhesive tape
- feather rubber stamp
- silver ink pad
- silver paper
- deckle-edged scissors

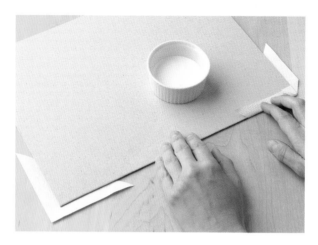

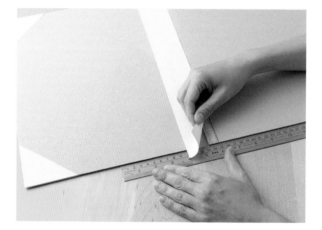

1 Cut two rectangles of straw board 33 x 25cm (13¼ x 10in). Use the template on page 101 to cut four triangles from cream leatherette paper, cutting along the solid lines. Mark the broken lines on the wrong side. Use PVA (white) glue to stick one triangle at either corner of one long edge of each board, matching the broken lines to the board edges. Glue the corners, then the paper edges over the boards.

2 Cut leatherette paper 36 x 5cm (14½ x 2in) for the hinge. Draw a pencil line 1.5cm (⅝in) in from the plain long edges of the boards on the right side. Glue one strip edge to one board, level with the drawn line and with 1.5cm (⅝in) extending at each end. Repeat with the other board, making sure the upper and lower board edges are level.

tip

It is often difficult to stamp motifs in a row. Place a ruler on the paper to butt the stamp against so that the motifs are applied level.

3 Turn the portfolio over and glue the extending ends to the inside. Cut leatherette paper 32 x 5cm (12⅞ x 2in). Glue to the underside of the hinge.

4 Refer to the diagram on page 101 to cut two covers from suede pile flock paper. Spread PVA (white) glue evenly on the wrong side. Stick the covers to the boards, overlapping the outer edges by 1.5cm (⅝in) and the triangles and hinge by 5mm (¼in). Glue the extending edges of the covers to the underside of the boards.

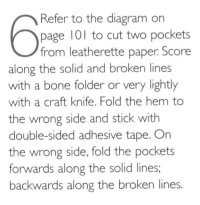

5 Cut a 2.5cm (1in) slit centrally 1.5cm (⅝in) from the long edges of the covers with a craft knife against a metal ruler, resting on a cutting mat. Cut the ribbon in half. Insert one length through each slit. Glue 1.5cm (⅝in) of the ends on the wrong side of the board. Glue two rectangles of speckled paper 32 × 24cm (12⅞ × 9⅝in) centrally to the wrong side of the portfolio.

6 Refer to the diagram on page 101 to cut two pockets from leatherette paper. Score along the solid and broken lines with a bone folder or very lightly with a craft knife. Fold the hem to the wrong side and stick with double-sided adhesive tape. On the wrong side, fold the pockets forwards along the solid lines; backwards along the broken lines.

7 Apply double-sided adhesive tape to the tabs of one pocket on the right side. Position the pocket on the inside of one cover inside the outer edges with the pocket opening facing inwards. Peel off the tape backing. Press in place. Repeat with the other pocket.

variation

To make this stylish pencil set, a strip of marbled paper has been applied around the shaft of ordinary lead pencils with art and hobby spray adhesive. A band of gold paper, one edge cut with deckle-edged scissors, has then been glued around the top of the pencils.

8 Stamp a row of three feathers onto speckled paper using a silver ink pad. Leave to dry. Cut out a rectangle around the feathers. Glue to a piece of silver paper. Trim the silver paper edges close to the speckled paper with deckle-edged scissors. Glue to the portfolio front.

honesty window collage

Handcrafted pictures are not just for displaying on a wall. Hang an eye-catching collage of translucent papers at a window to create a focal point of interest and at the same time conceal an unattractive view or bring privacy to an interior. This delightful window panel is inspired by the natural world with its delicate images of honesty seed heads complete with seeds, a hovering dragonfly and wind-blown seeds.

The collage pieces are applied to a background of fine Japanese papers and outlined with pearlized relief paints. The panel is bordered by a scalloped frame of pearlized silver card. Metal eyelets at the top of the frame allow the panel to be suspended on ribbons.

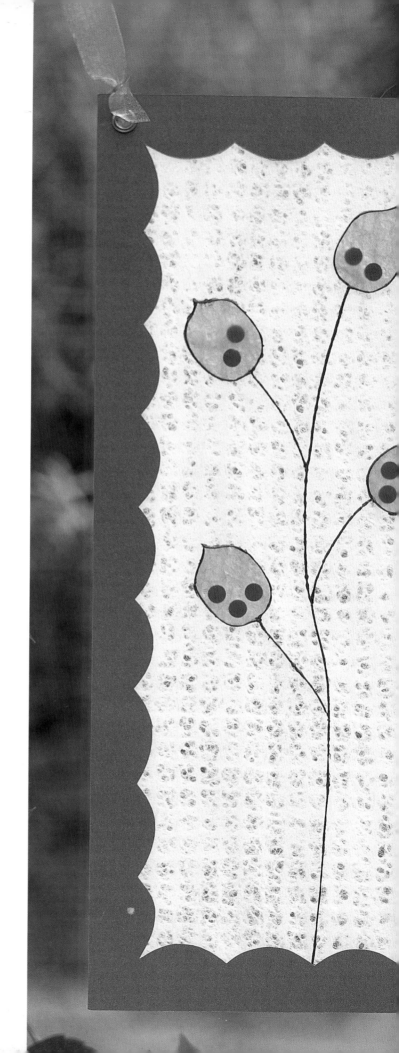

honesty window collage

you will need

- white translucent grid-patterned paper
- holepunch
- silver pearlized card
- cocktail stick (toothpick)
- PVA (white) glue
- lilac and blue translucent papers, e.g. transparent satin
- spray mount adhesive
- grey translucent textured paper, e.g. Japanese hikakushi
- white translucent spiral-patterned paper
- blue, light green and lilac pearlized relief paints
- plastic spreader, glue brush or scrap of card, for applying glue
- awl
- 2 metal eyelets
- eyelet fixing tool

tip

To hang the panel on a wall rather than at a window, simply stick the framed panel onto white card with spray mount adhesive.

1 Enlarge the template on page 102. Cut a 28 x 13cm (11 x 5⅛in) rectangle from white translucent grid-patterned paper. Place the rectangle on the template over the honesty rectangle. For the seeds, use a holepunch to punch nine circles from silver pearlized card. Use a cocktail stick to apply PVA (white) glue sparingly to the circles and stick them to the white paper within the seed head outlines, placing two or three seeds within each seed head.

2 Refer to the same template to cut four honesty seed heads from lilac translucent paper. Stick the seed heads in place with spray mount adhesive, covering the seeds.

3 Refer to the template to cut the dragonfly body from blue translucent paper and the dragonfly wings from grey textured translucent paper. Cut a 17 x 15.5cm (6¾ x 6⅛in) rectangle from white translucent spiral-patterned paper. Place the rectangle on the template over the dragonfly rectangle. Arrange the dragonfly pieces in position, placing the body over the base of the wings. Stick the pieces in place with spray mount adhesive.

4 Outline the honesty seed heads and draw the stems with blue pearlized relief paint. Outline the dragonfly with light green pearlized relief paint. Cut a 15.5 × 12cm (6⅛ × 4¾in) rectangle from white translucent grid-patterned paper. Place the rectangle over the lower rectangle on the template and draw the wind-blown seeds with lilac pearlized relief paint. Set aside to dry.

5 Refer to the template to cut the frame from silver pearlized card. Cut out the windows for the decorated rectangles using a craft knife, resting on a cutting mat. Cut the straight edges against a metal ruler. Glue the rectangles to the back of the frame with PVA (white) glue using a plastic spreader, glue brush or a scrap of card.

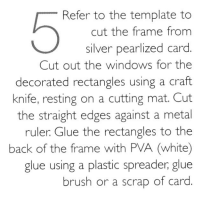

variation

This pretty greetings card is appropriate for all kinds of occasions. The fluttering dragonfly is cut from blue translucent papers and outlined with gold pearlized relief paint.

6 Pierce a hole in the frame at the dots with an awl. Make the holes large enough to accommodate the eyelets. Fix an eyelet through each hole with the fixing tool, following the manufacturer's instructions.

paisley table decorations

Keen crafters usually have more than one skill up their sleeve, and this colourful project combines paper crafts with the equally popular art of embroidery. A bold paisley design is pinpricked and the resulting holes embroidered with vibrant stranded cotton embroidery threads. Even if you have no experience of sewing, the design is very simple to work. The stitches used are backstitch, straight stitch and lazy daisy stitch.

Celebration dinners deserve special accessories such as these place-names and small gift boxes. The place-name holders are reusable – a metallic-strip fastening holds a rectangle of card on which the guest's name is written in place inside the holder. Adhesive magnetic strip is available from craft stores or suppliers. The gift box will make a treasured memento of a meaningful occasion.

paisley table decorations

you will need

- pink and orange card
- bone folder (optional)
- compasses
- crewel embroidery needle
- stranded cotton embroidery thread
- adhesive magnetic strip
- cream card
- double-sided adhesive tape

1 **To make the place-name holder**, trace the template on page 103 onto tracing paper and transfer onto pink or orange card. Cut out. Score the broken lines on the right side with a bone folder or craft knife against a metal ruler. Tape the tracing to the holder with masking tape. Resting on a cutting mat, prick the dots with the point of the compasses. Remove the tracing.

2 Thread the needle with six strands of orange embroidery thread for a pink holder, cream for an orange holder. Knot the ends. To backstitch along the centre line, bring the needle to the right side through a hole second from the top on the outline. Insert it through the previous hole and bring it out through the following hole. Continue along the centre line. Work the 'arms' in straight stitches.

tip

If you make a mistake in the stitching or decide to change the colour of your threads, just unthread the holes and start again.

3 Work backstitch along the paisley outline with lime green thread on a pink holder, magenta on orange.

4 To work lazy daisy stitches outwards from the paisley, bring the needle to the right side through an inner hole. Insert it back through the same hole, leaving a loop of threads on the right side. Bring the needle to the right side through the outer hole, through the loop. Pull the threads to anchor the loop, then insert the needle back through the outer hole. Use cream thread on a pink holder, blue on orange.

5 Fold the holder backwards along the scored lines. Cut two 1.5cm (⅝in) pieces of magnetic strip. Peel off the backing tapes and stick centrally to the inside opening edges of the holder. Cut a 10 × 6cm (4 × 2¼in) rectangle of cream card on which to write the name. Slip the left edge inside the holder and close.

6 To make the gift box, trace the lid template on page 103 onto tracing paper and use to cut a lid from pink or orange card. Follow the box side diagram on page 102 to cut a box side from pink or orange card. On the right side, score the broken lines with a bone folder or craft knife against a metal ruler. Embroider the lid with the paisley design and the lid sides with random lazy daisy stitches using lime green thread for a pink box, magenta for orange. Fold the lid backwards along the scored lines. Follow step 3 on page 32 to construct the lid.

7 Embroider the box side with random lazy daisy stitches using lime green thread for a pink box, magenta for orange, keeping the stitches 2cm (¾in) below the upper edge. Fold backwards along the scored lines. Apply double-sided adhesive tape to the base tabs on the wrong side and the end tab on the right side. Cut a 9.4 × 7.4cm (3⁷⁄₁₆ × 2⅞in) rectangle of card for the base. Follow step 5 on page 33 to complete the box.

variation

A change of colour gives a completely different look to the place-name holder and gift box. Here, card is covered with cream echizen washi paper, which is peppered with tiny gold and silver fragments. The paisley design is then embroidered with golden thread.

65

celtic mosaic casket

It is the superb printed metallic papers used to create this regal box that make this design so effective. Two techniques are employed – découpage, the Victorian craft of applying paper cuts, which are then varnished with many coats to seal the surface, and mosaic work using paper instead of pieces of ceramic or glass.

Lightweight papers realistically printed to resemble copper and aluminium are applied to a wooden box painted with a simple pewter effect. Plain wooden box blanks are available for decoration by mail order and from craft stores. Simple motifs work best for this paper mosaic technique. The Celtic knotwork on the lid represents an eternal union, making the box an appropriately symbolic wedding gift. A plain border on the sides of the box prevents the design from becoming over-fussy.

celtic mosaic casket

you will need

- wooden box with lid, 19 x 11.5cm (7½ x 4½in) and 11.5 cm (4½in) high
- black and silver acrylic paint
- palette or old plate
- 2.5cm (1in) flat paintbrush
- copper acrylic paint (optional)
- copper-effect paper
- aluminium-effect paper
- sheet of plastic, e.g. cut from a plastic carrier bag
- PVA (white) glue
- old paintbrush, for applying glue
- kitchen towel
- clear satin polyurethane varnish
- 3cm (1¼in) flat paintbrush
- fine glasspaper

tip

Do not worry about placing the mosaic pieces very precisely. As long as there is a gap between the pieces, they will resemble real mosaic work.

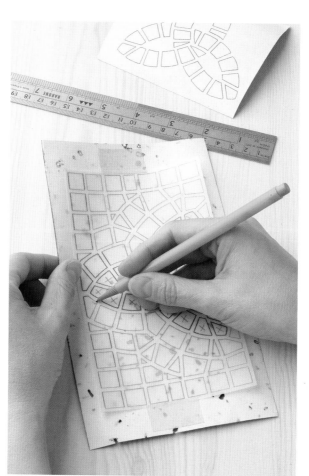

1 Blend black and silver acrylic paint together on a palette or an old plate. Use to paint the exterior of the lid and box with a flat paintbrush. Leave to dry. Paint the interior of the lid and box with the silver acrylic paint. If the lid and box have mouldings, paint them with copper acrylic paint. Leave to dry.

2 Trace the lid and box templates on pages 104–105 onto tracing paper with a pencil. Mark the shaded sections. Tape the tracings right side down on the wrong side of the relevant metallic papers with masking tape: copper for the shaded sections and aluminium for the other sections. Redraw the templates to transfer the designs. Make one tracing for the sides and one for the front and back of the box. Remove the tracings.

3 Tape the lid tracing to the lid along one edge with masking tape as a guide to positioning the pieces. With scissors, cut out a few of the mosaic pieces at a time as you use them, so that they don't become muddled. Working on two or three pieces at a time, lay the mosaic pieces wrong side up on a sheet of plastic. Paste the wrong side of the pieces with PVA (white) glue. Lift the tracing and slip the pieces underneath. Press in position. Wipe off the excess glue with moistened kitchen towel. Stick all the lid pieces to the lid.

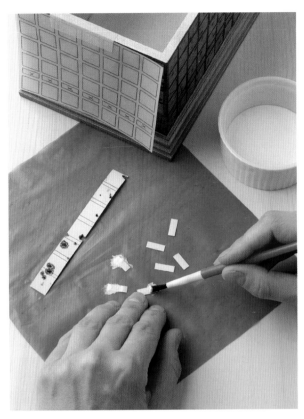

4 Tape the box side tracing to one side of the box along one edge with masking tape. Cut out and paste the wrong side of the pieces with glue, then stick in place. Repeat on all sides of the box.

5 Remove the tracings and allow the glue to dry for a day. Coat the exterior of the lid and box with varnish. Leave to dry. Apply a further five coats of varnish, sanding lightly between the last two coats.

variation

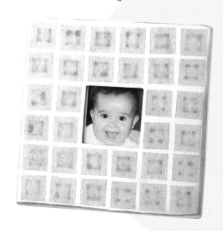

Apply squares of metallic paper freehand to a metal picture frame to give it a contemporary feel. Varnish the frame if you wish, although since it won't be handled often, the frame can be left unvarnished.

paper sculpture animals

Basic paper-folding techniques are applied here to make these majestic creatures. The cats fold flat, so they can be used as greetings cards with a message written on the underside. Each animal is cut from a sheet of writing paper, which comes in a wide range of colours and is often available in single sheets from stationery stores or suppliers. The facial features and tiger's markings are drawn with a fine felt pen and the lion's wonderful shaggy mane is cut with small, pointed scissors. Curling the mane fringes over closed scissor blades really adds to the three-dimensional quality of the lion.

Simply change the tiger's markings to make a leopard or a cheetah, or make a cat to resemble a favourite feline pet by using a suitably coloured paper and painting on realistic stripes or tortoiseshell markings.

paper sculpture animals

you will need

- amber paper, 120gsm in weight
- beige paper, 120gsm in weight
- fine black felt pen
- small, pointed scissors
- fawn paper, 120gsm in weight
- PVA (white) glue
- cocktail stick (toothpick)

1 Trace the cat and ear template on page 106 onto tracing paper with a pencil. Tape the tracing face down on amber paper for a tiger and beige paper for a lion using masking tape. Redraw the cat outline and ear to transfer them. Transfer the facial features and markings to the tiger, and the facial features only to the lion. Turn the tracing over and tape in place to transfer the other half and ear.

2 Remove the tracing. Draw the facial features and markings with a fine black felt pen. Cut out the cats and ears. Lightly score along the solid and broken lines with a craft knife against a metal ruler, resting on a cutting mat, and cut the ear slits.

3 To make the tiger, cut away small 'V' shapes around the head with the scissors to suggest fur. Fold the head and body lengthways in half, then fold along the broken lines with the right sides facing and along the solid lines with the wrong sides facing, tucking the broken lines under the head and the base of the tail under the end of the body.

tip

When trimming the fringe ends for the lion's mane, cut some of them shorter to give the mane an untamed appearance.

4 Poke the straight end of each ear through the slits for 5mm (¼in) and glue to the underside of the head.

5 **To make the lion**, follow steps 3 and 4 to fold the head and body, and insert the ears. Cut a rectangle of amber paper 16 × 4cm (6¼ × 1½in) for a short mane. Refer to the template on page 106 to cut a long mane from fawn paper. Lightly score along the centre of both manes with a craft knife, parallel with the long edges. Fold in half along the scored line. Use the scissors to cut a fringe along the long edges through both thicknesses to within 2mm (⅟₁₆in) of the fold.

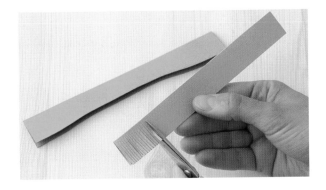

6 Fan the fringes outwards from the fold between your fingers. Gently pull the ends over the closed scissor blades to curl the fringe. Run a line of PVA (white) glue under the edges of the head using a cocktail stick. Stick the folded edge of the short mane under the head with the fringe curling forwards. Trim the fringe ends to a point.

7 Run a line of PVA (white) glue under the edges of the head using a cocktail stick. Starting under the chin, stick the folded edge of the long mane under the head with the fringe curling forwards. Trim the fringe as before.

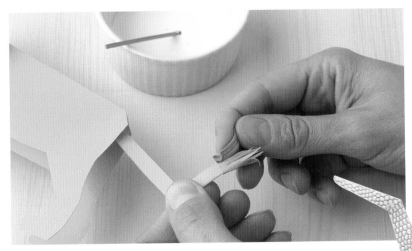

variation

Use the template on page 106 to cut this slithering snake's body and head from snakeskin-effect paper and tongue from red paper. Fold the pieces lengthways in half, then fold along the broken lines with right sides facing and along the solid lines with wrong sides facing, tucking the broken lines under the solid lines. Glue the head to the body and the tongue under the head. Draw the eyes with a fine black pen.

8 Cut amber paper 4 × 2cm (1½ × ¾in) for the tail tip. Lightly score along the centre with a craft knife, parallel with the short edges. Fold in half along the scored line. Cut a fringe along the edges through both thicknesses to within 2mm (⅟₁₆in) of the fold. Trim the fringe ends to a point. Fold the end of the tail in half with right sides facing. Wrap the tail tip around the end of the tail and stick in place.

oriental concertina notebooks

These practical concertina notebooks have a flavour of the East in more ways than one. The notebooks are covered with echizen washi paper, which is a Japanese paper, and the stamped design of cranes and bamboo are favourite oriental motifs. The notebooks even fasten with chopsticks, and the choice of the colour red symbolizes joy and celebration in China.

The pages open in a concertina fashion and can be written on both sides or used as a scrapbook for mounting and preserving precious souvenirs and cherished mementos. Loops of fine leather or cotton thonging wrap around the books to keep them neatly closed and are then secured in place with a coordinating chopstick.

oriental concertina notebooks

you will need

- oriental rubber stamp
- red ink pad
- beige paper
- thin card
- decorative red or beige paper, e.g. echizen washi
- PVA (white) glue
- glue brush, plastic spreader or scrap of card, for applying glue
- old newspapers
- 1.5cm (⅝in) chisel and hammer or mallet (optional)
- 80cm (⅞yd) beige or red leather or cotton thonging
- beige or red paper, 120–140gsm in weight
- bone folder (optional)
- one 18cm (7in) beige or red chopstick

tip

Consider using other fastenings. A sturdy twig would compliment a stamped leaf motif. Alternatively, a brightly coloured pen would coordinate with a bold, modern design.

1 Gently press the rubber stamp onto the ink pad. Stamp the motif onto beige paper. Allow to dry. Cut out a rectangle or square around the motif leaving a margin of 1.5cm (⅝in).

2 Cut two rectangles of thin card 20 x 11cm (8 x 4⅜in) using a craft knife against a metal ruler, resting on a cutting mat. On one rectangle, which will form the front, cut out a window for the stamped motif 1cm (⅜in) wider on all sides than the motif.

3 For the covers, cut two rectangles of decorative paper 23 x 14cm (9¼ x 5⅝in) using a craft knife against a metal ruler, resting on a cutting mat. Place the card rectangles centrally on the wrong side of the papers. Glue the corners, then the edges of the paper over the card pieces using PVA (white) glue.

4 Cut the paper inside the window to within 1.5cm (⅝in) of the edges. Snip the paper to the window corners. Fold the paper over the window edges and glue to the underside of the card. Leave to dry. Glue the stamped motif behind the window.

5 Resting on old newspapers, punch a 1.5cm (⅝in) long slit on the right side of the front 1.5cm (⅝in) in from the right-hand edge and 8cm (3¼in) above the lower edge by holding a chisel upright on the front and hitting it with a hammer or mallet. Alternatively, cut the slit with a craft knife against a metal ruler, resting on a cutting mat.

6 Cut a 6.5cm (2½in) and a 68cm (26¾in) length of thonging. Bend the short length in half to form a loop. Insert the ends through the slit from the right side. Lay the ends side by side on the wrong side.

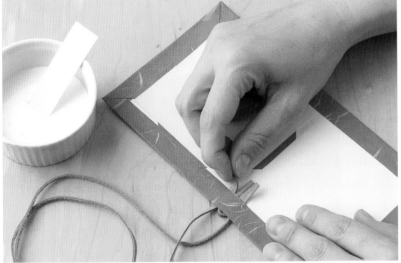

7 Insert the ends of the long length through the slit from the right side, forming a long loop. Lay each end either side of the short ends on the wrong side. Adjust the thronging so that the ends extend for 1.5cm (⅝in) on the wrong side. Glue the ends to the underside of the front.

variation

Here, a plain gift box has been covered with colourful origami papers. For the gift tag, cut a length of plain paper, fold it in concertina folds and stamp a design on the top. Sprinkle embossing powder on the motif and hold it over a heat source to melt the powder. Tie to the gift with gold cord.

8 Cut a strip of beige or red paper 63 × 19.5cm (26¼ × 7¾in). Score across the length at 11cm (4⅜in) intervals with a bone folder or lightly with a craft knife. Fold the scored lines in alternate directions to create the concertina pages. Spread glue on the back page and stick centrally to the wrong side of the back cover. Spread glue on the front page and press the front cover on top, lining it up with the back cover. To fasten, wrap the long loop of thonging around the notebook and over the short loop. Slip the chopstick through the short loop.

photograph transfer box

Protect favourite photographs and mementos of a cherished child in a specially personalized container. This box is covered with beautiful handmade paper embedded with rich, magenta-coloured leaves.

The picture is from a photograph that has been transferred onto a tactile ridged card for added interest. Transfer paper, which is available from art and graphic stores or suppliers, allows images to be transferred onto all sorts of surfaces including textured card. Simply take your chosen picture, in this case a baby photograph, to a photocopy shop for it to be photocopied onto the transfer paper, then follow the manufacturer's instructions to transfer the image onto textured card. The picture is applied to the box lid using handcrafted photo mounts.

photograph transfer box

you will need

- handmade paper embedded with leaves or petals
- thin card
- art and hobby spray adhesive
- bone folder (optional)
- double-sided adhesive tape
- photograph
- transfer paper
- white thin ridged card
- PVA (white) glue
- plastic spreader, glue brush or scrap of card, for applying glue
- sponge
- pewter pearlized card

tip

When making your choice of photograph, bear in mind that the finished picture will be a mirror image of the original.

1 Apply a sheet of handmade paper to thin card with art and hobby spray adhesive to strengthen it. Copy the lid diagram on page 105 onto tracing paper and use as a template to cut a lid from the mounted handmade paper with a craft knife, resting on a cutting mat. Remove the tracing. On the wrong side, score along the broken lines with a bone folder or craft knife against a metal ruler. Fold the lid forwards along the scored lines to form the lid shape.

2 Apply double-sided adhesive tape to the lid tabs on the right side. Peel off the backing tapes and stick under the opposite ends of the lid sides.

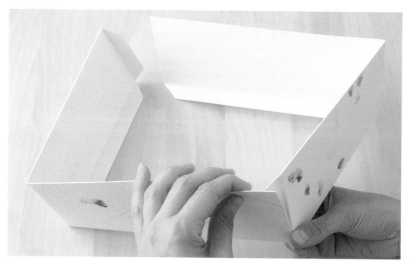

3 Refer to the diagram on page 105 to cut two box sides from the mounted handmade paper. On the wrong side, score along the broken lines with a bone folder or craft knife against a metal ruler. Fold forwards along the scored lines. Apply double-sided adhesive tape to the end tabs on the right side and the base tabs on the wrong side. Peel the backing tapes off one end tab and stick under the straight end of the other box side.

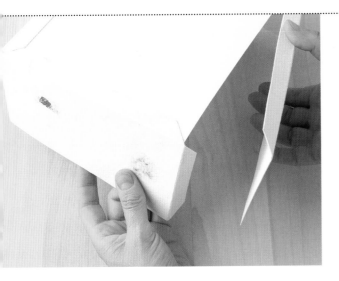

4 Roughly cut out a 21.5 × 16.5cm (8½ × 6⅜in) rectangle of the thin card for the base. Peel the backing tapes off the remaining tabs and stick the base tabs under the base. Stick the end tab under the opposite end of the box side.

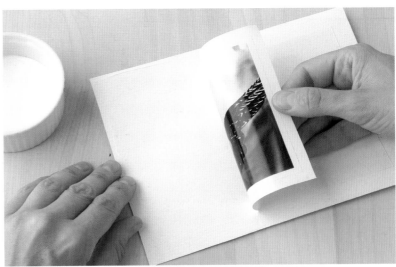

5 Following the manufacturer's instructions, have your photograph photocopied onto transfer paper. Cut out the image. Cut a piece of white ridged card about 2cm (¾in) larger all round than the photocopied image. Coat the right side of the card with PVA (white) glue using a plastic spreader, glue brush or a scrap of card. Stick the image face down on the glue, smoothing it outwards from the centre.

6 Wet the paper backing of the image with a moistened sponge. Peel off the paper backing to reveal the image. Smooth it onto the card securely and leave to dry. Cut out the picture.

variation

Heirloom wedding photographs are photocopied and applied to the front of cards of folded handmade paper with ready-made photo mounts to commemorate special anniversaries.

7 Using the template on page 105, cut four photo mounts from pewter pearlized card with a craft knife, resting on a cutting mat, then cut the slits. Slip the corners of the picture into the mounts. Glue the mounts to the lid with PVA (white) glue.

flower party lights

Turn plain fairy lights into glamorous illuminated flowers to bring style and vitality to a party venue. The flowers are custom-made to fit your particular lightbulbs and are simple to construct, so it is practical to create a whole mass of them for a high-impact, elaborate effect. Interestingly textured papers in vibrant colours have been used here – either choose a single shade or use a rainbow of colours to match the revelling mood of the party. But why wait for a celebration when you can drape them across a wall or curtain pelmet to brighten up a bedroom.

The curled petals are easily achieved by wrapping the tips around the handle of a fine artist's paintbrush. Each flower also has a pretty leaf attached.

flower party lights

you will need

- scrap paper or card
- orange textured paper
- thin orange card
- all-purpose household glue
- lime green textured paper
- fairy lights
- fine artist's paintbrush
- adhesive putty
  (blu-tack) (optional)

1 Refer to the template on page 97 to cut a template of scrap paper or card to cut flowers from orange textured paper. Cut a circle of thin orange card for each flower. Glue each circle to the centre of the underside of each flower using all-purpose household glue.

2 Use the template on page 97 to cut a leaf for each flower from green textured paper. Fold the leaves lengthways in half to make a central 'vein', then open them out flat again. Glue the rounded end of each leaf to the circle of each flower.

tip

Experiment with different shaped petals for the flowers. For instance, daisy- or poppy-like petals would look very attractive. The leaves can be omitted if you wish.

3 The central star on the flower is cut to make slits through which to insert the lightbulb. Measure the diameter of the lightbulbs of your fairy lights. The slits given on the template are for a 1.5cm (⅝in) diameter lightbulb. If your lightbulb is not this size, draw each slit half the diameter measurement of your lightbulb, so that the flower fits over it. Place the template on the flower and use a craft knife, resting on a cutting mat, to cut the slits.

4 Overlap one petal over the next by approximately 4mm (³⁄₁₆in) at the widest part and glue in place. Repeat on all the petals, to form a cup shape.

5 Wrap each petal tip around the handle of a fine artist's paintbrush to curl it under. Alternatively, leave the petals uncurled if you prefer.

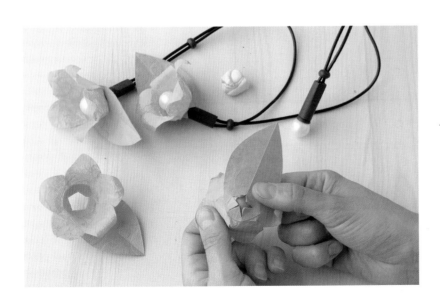

Variation

Cut a flower from brightly coloured paper and cut out a circle in the centre for inserting a candle. Overlap the petals and glue them together. Slip the flower over a candle to make a charming table decoration.

6 Push the slits open by inserting your finger or thumb into the flower. Push the lightbulb up through the flower. The lightbulbs must not touch the flower when they are lit, so it is advisable to secure each flower in place with a little adhesive putty under the leaf.

swedish embossed stationery

Embossing paper with simple motifs is known nowadays as parchment craft and is very popular, since professional results are quickly achieved. Ready-made stencils are available by mail order to emboss through but it is easy to make your own from stencil sheet or thick card. Stencil sheet is recommended because it is more hard-wearing than thick card. Specialist embossing tools are also available, or improvise by using the rounded handle end of a fine artist's paintbrush.

This selection of stationery uses traditional Swedish motifs of a stylized bird and flower. Embossed on red paper, they look suitably festive to use for Christmas correspondence. The writing paper and greetings cards are trimmed with ordinary brown parcel paper cut with pinking shears, and the greeting cards are made from coordinating corrugated card.

swedish embossed stationery

you will need

- stencil sheet or thick card
- red writing paper
- small ball embossing tool or fine artist's paintbrush
- brown parcel paper
- pinking shears
- spray mount adhesive
- brown corrugated card

1 Refer to the templates on page 106 to cut the bird and flower motifs from stencil sheet or thick card with a craft knife, resting on a cutting mat.

2 **To make the embossed writing paper,** position the stencil at the top of the right side of the red writing paper. Tape in place with masking tape.

Refer to the templates on page 106

tip

Art stores or suppliers sell coloured corrugated card. Alternatively, spray-paint corrugated card packaging in the colour of your choice.

3 Turn the paper over and rub through the stencil with a small ball embossing tool or the handle end of a fine artist's paintbrush. The design will be embossed on the right side. Move the stencil along the paper and repeat to stencil more motifs. Turn the bird stencil over to make a mirror image.

4 Cut strips of brown parcel paper 8mm–1cm (5⁄16in–3⁄8in) wide, cutting one edge with a pair of pinking shears. Stick the strip just inside the top or left-hand edge with spray mount adhesive. Cut the ends of the strips level with the paper.

5 To make the embossed greetings card, cut a 20cm (8in) square of brown corrugated card. Fold in half parallel with the corrugations. Emboss a row of three motifs on red paper. Cut the paper to form a rectangle. Stick the embossed rectangle to brown parcel paper with spray mount adhesive. Trim the paper, leaving a 5mm (1⁄4in) border.

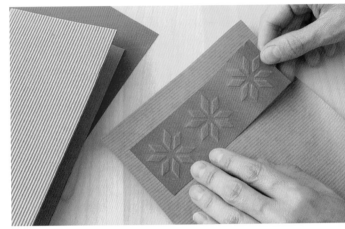

variation

Create a matching seal to deliver your embossed stationery in style. Emboss a motif on a rectangle of paper and apply it to a piece of contrasting coloured paper. Cut around the motif with pinking shears and stick it to the envelope flap.

6 Stick the rectangle onto red paper and cut a similar border with straight scissors or pinking shears. Stick to the front of the card with spray mount adhesive. If you wish, cut two strips of red paper, cutting one edge with pinking shears. Stick the strips across each end of the card front with spray mount adhesive. Cut the ends of the strips level with the paper.

translucent christmas baubles

Adorn a Christmas tree or arrangement of twigs for the festive season with an array of vibrant baubles. These dainty decorations are made of translucent paper that allows the light to shine through. The baubles are enriched with glitter and pearlized relief paints, which comes in a tube or a plastic bottle and is applied via a fine nozzle. In this case, the decorative designs consist of dots of relief paint, but you could draw lines if you prefer.

As a finishing touch, the baubles are flamboyantly suspended on coloured wires coiled into spirals, which can be slipped onto Christmas tree branches or twigs. Alternatively, to hang them at a window, simply fasten fishing line or fine thread to the spirals.

translucent christmas baubles

you will need

- selection of translucent papers, e.g. transparent satin
- PVA (white) glue
- cocktail stick (toothpick)
- glitter relief paints
- pearlized relief paints
- thick needle
- 1mm diameter coloured wire
- wire cutters or an old pair of scissors
- jewellery pliers
- fishing line or fine thread (optional)

1 Trace the bauble templates on page 100 onto translucent papers. For some of the baubles, trace the flowers onto contrasting coloured translucent paper. Cut out the flowers with a craft knife, resting on a cutting mat, or with a pair of scissors. Apply PVA (white) glue sparingly to the centre of the flowers with a cocktail stick. Stick the flowers to the baubles.

tip

Avoid using paper that is very thin and likely to flop for making these decorations. Here, transparent satin paper with a weight of 200gsm was used.

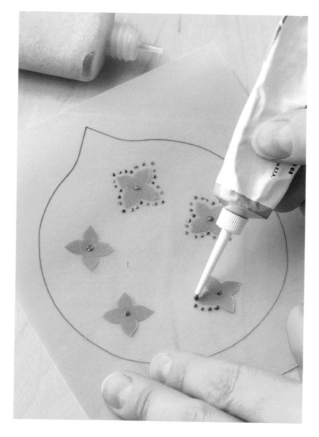

2 Decorate the baubles freehand by applying dots of glitter and pearlized relief paints. Set them aside to dry. Cut the baubles out with a craft knife, resting on a cutting mat, or with a pair of scissors.

3 Pierce a hole in each bauble at the dot with a thick needle. Snip a 14cm (5½in) length of coloured wire for each bauble. Using a pair of jewellery pliers, bend one end of each length of wire into a hook to suspend the baubles.

4 Bend the other end of each length of wire, at a right angle to the hook, between your fingers to form a spiral.

5 Slip the hook through the hole in the bauble and squeeze it closed with the jewellery pliers. If hanging at a window, tie a length of fishing line or fine thread to the spiral of each bauble.

variation

Cut a 25 x 12.5cm (10 x 5in) rectangle of card. Score and fold a 10cm (4in) base from one short end. Open flat and cut out a bauble on the front. Glue translucent paper behind the cutout and adorn with relief paint. Refold once dry. Cut two brackets (page 100) – score and fold along the broken lines. Glue to the base and front at each side. Slip gold thread through the top and tie. Sit a nightlight (tealight) on the base.

NB: never leave a lighted candle unattended

templates & diagrams

All templates are full-size unless otherwise stated.

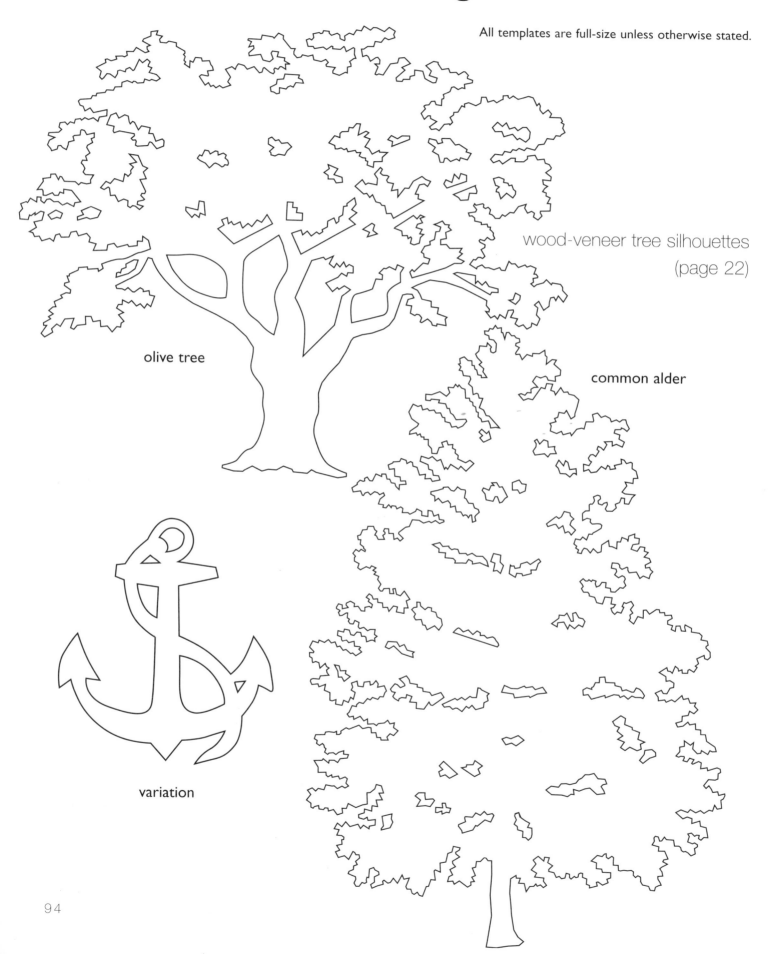

wood-veneer tree silhouettes
(page 22)

olive tree

common alder

variation

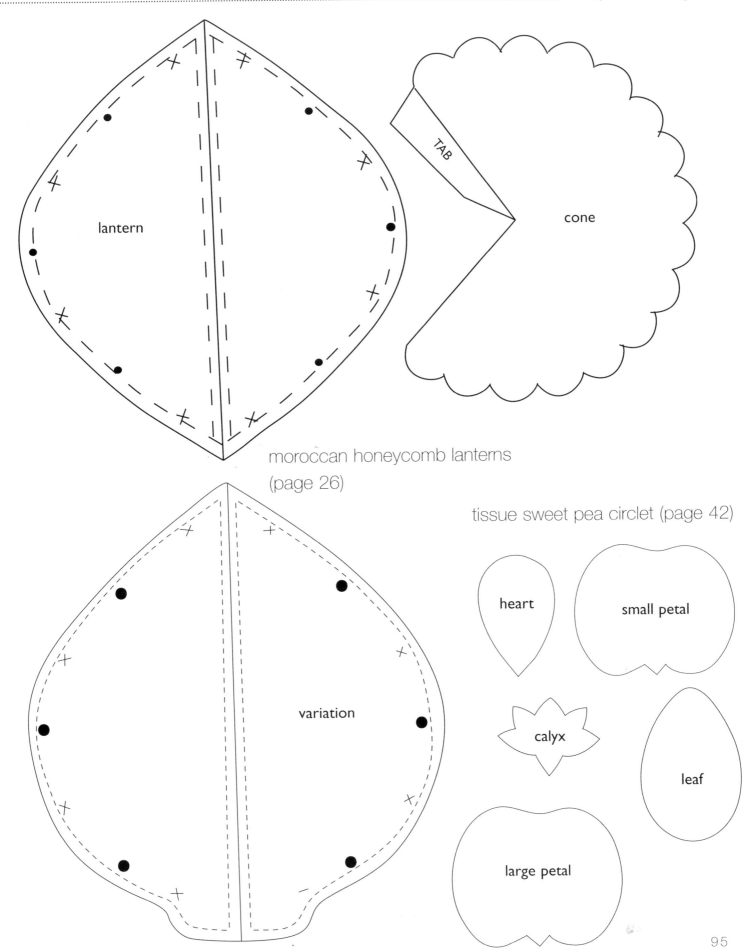

lantern

cone

TAB

moroccan honeycomb lanterns
(page 26)

tissue sweet pea circlet (page 42)

variation

heart

small petal

calyx

leaf

large petal

pinpricked wedding gift box (page 30)

gift box lid
enlarge by 133%

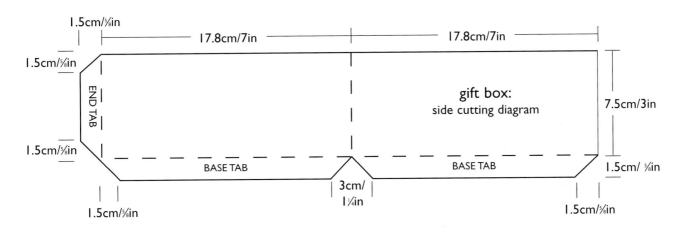

1.5cm/⅝in

17.8cm/7in

17.8cm/7in

1.5cm/⅝in

END TAB

gift box:
side cutting diagram

7.5cm/3in

1.5cm/⅝in

BASE TAB

BASE TAB

1.5cm/ ⅝in

3cm/
1¼in

1.5cm/⅝in

1.5cm/⅝in

gift enclosure

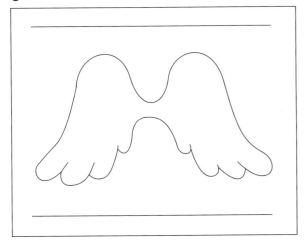

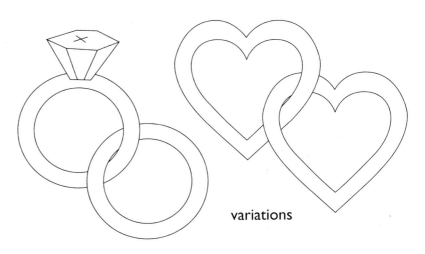

variations

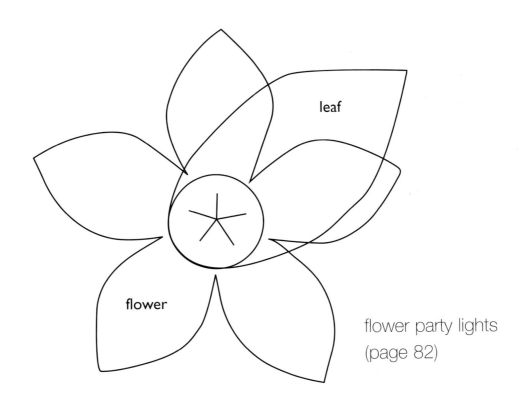

leaf

flower

flower party lights
(page 82)

embellished origami boxes (page 38)

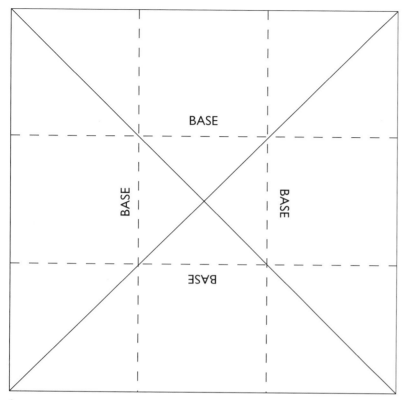

BASE

BASE

BASE

BASE

box

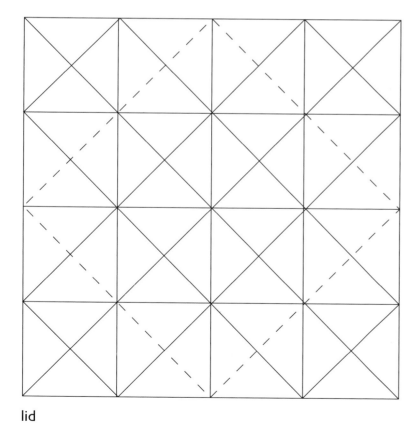

lid

embroidered & glitter albums (page 34)

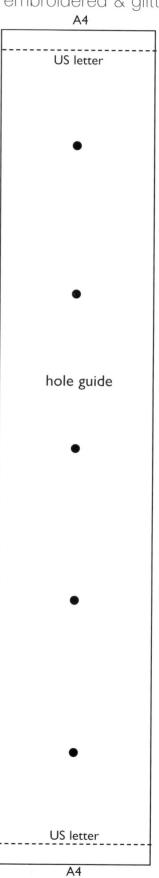

A4

US letter

hole guide

US letter

A4

fern & leaf desk accessories (page 46)

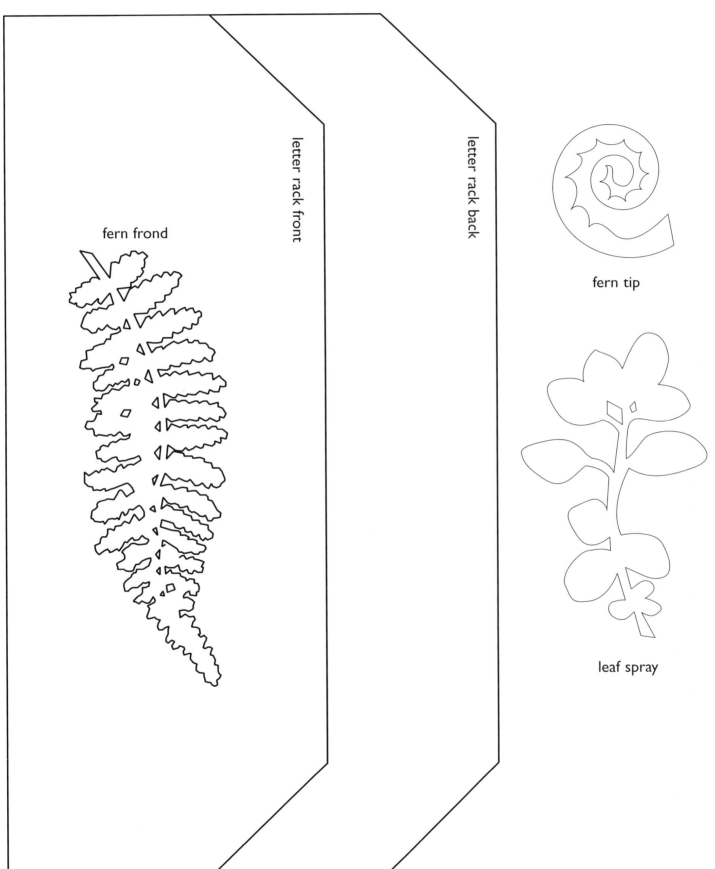

letter rack front

letter rack back

fern frond

fern tip

leaf spray

fern & leaf desk accessories (page 46)

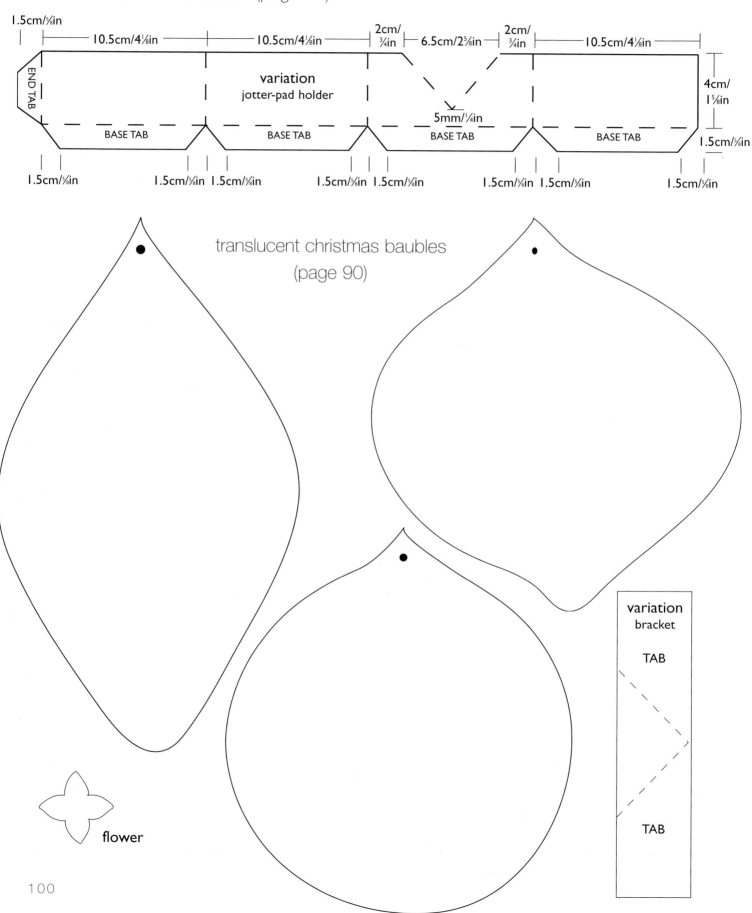

1.5cm/⅝in

10.5cm/4⅛in — 10.5cm/4⅛in — 2cm/¾in — 6.5cm/2⅝in — 2cm/¾in — 10.5cm/4⅛in

END TAB

variation
jotter-pad holder

4cm/1⅝in

BASE TAB   BASE TAB   BASE TAB   BASE TAB

5mm/¼in

1.5cm/⅝in

1.5cm/⅝in   1.5cm/⅝in 1.5cm/⅝in   1.5cm/⅝in 1.5cm/⅝in   1.5cm/⅝in 1.5cm/⅝in   1.5cm/⅝in

translucent christmas baubles
(page 90)

variation
bracket

TAB

TAB

flower

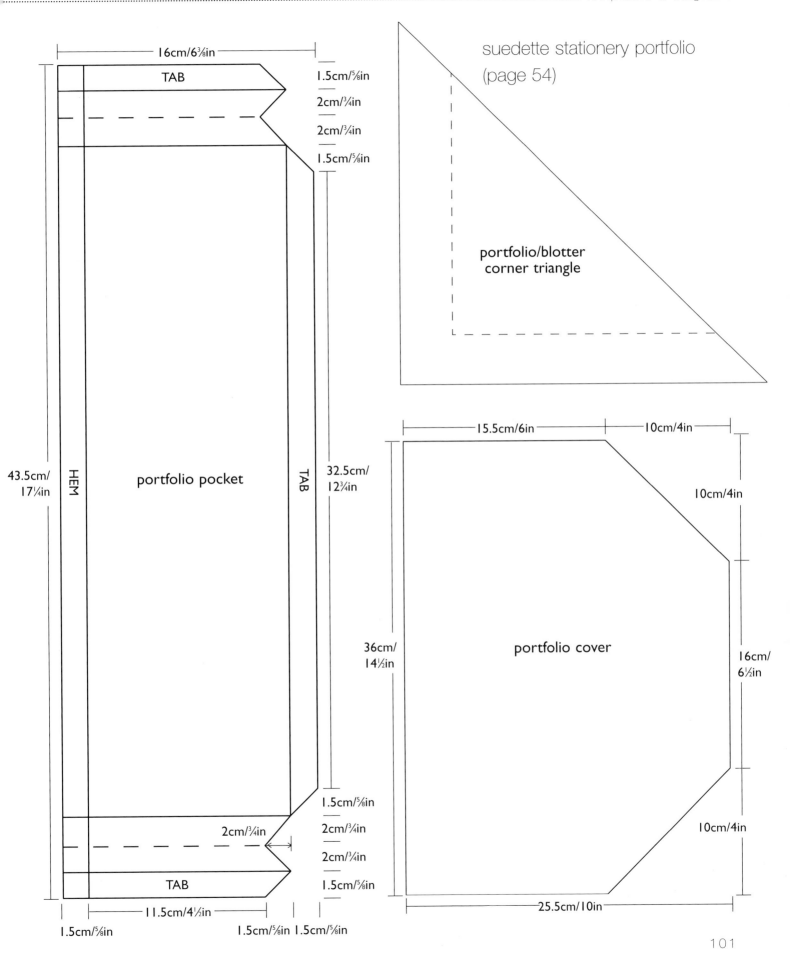

16cm/6⅜in

TAB

1.5cm/⅝in

2cm/¾in

2cm/¾in

1.5cm/⅝in

suedette stationery portfolio
(page 54)

portfolio/blotter
corner triangle

43.5cm/
17¼in

HEM

portfolio pocket

TAB

32.5cm/
12¾in

15.5cm/6in

10cm/4in

10cm/4in

36cm/
14½in

portfolio cover

16cm/
6½in

1.5cm/⅝in

2cm/¾in

2cm/¾in

1.5cm/⅝in

2cm/¾in

TAB

11.5cm/4½in

10cm/4in

25.5cm/10in

1.5cm/⅝in

1.5cm/⅝in 1.5cm/⅝in

honesty window collage (page 58) **enlarge by 200%**

paisley table decorations (page 62)

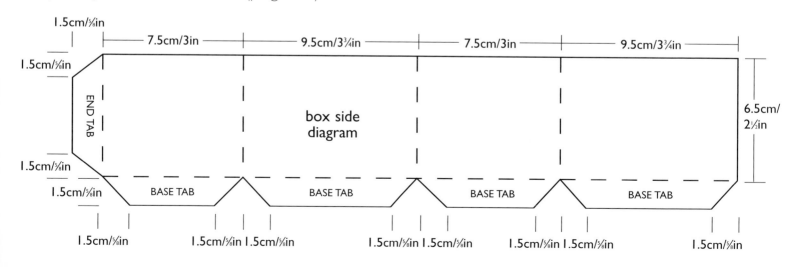

paisley table decorations (page 62)

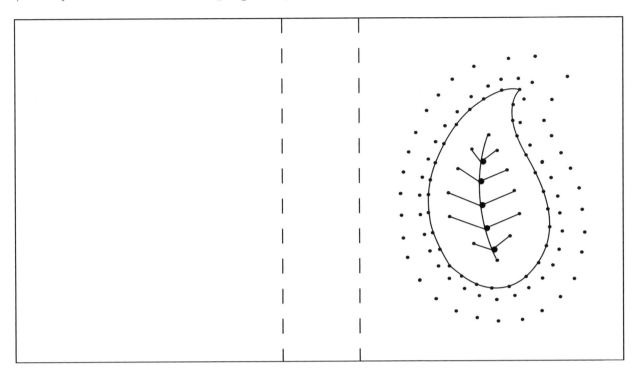

place-name holder

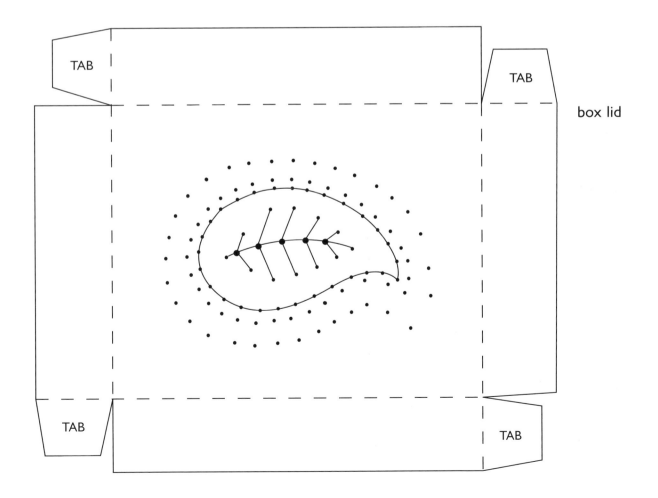

box lid

celtic mosaic casket (page 66)

lid

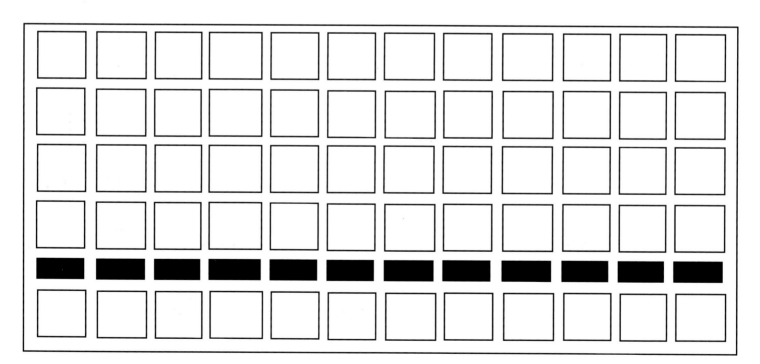

front and back

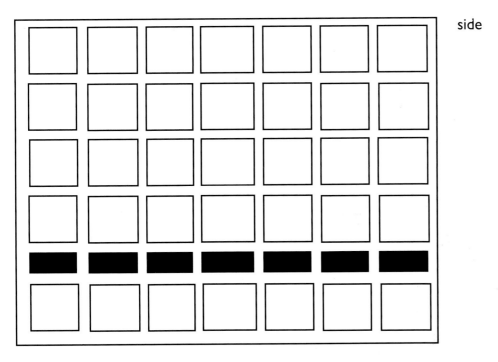

side

photograph transfer box
(page 78)

photo mount

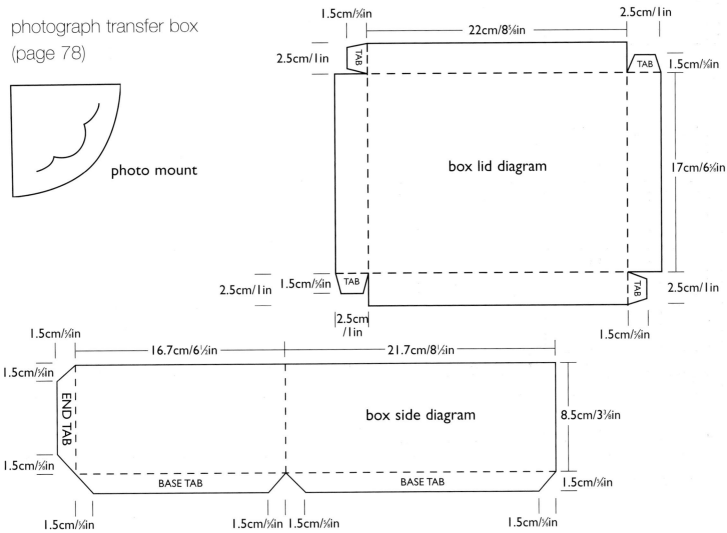

1.5cm/⅝in

2.5cm/1in

2.5cm/1in

22cm/8⅝in

TAB

TAB

1.5cm/⅝in

box lid diagram

17cm/6⅝in

2.5cm/1in

1.5cm/⅝in

TAB

TAB

2.5cm/1in

2.5cm/1in

1.5cm/⅝in

1.5cm/⅝in

1.5cm/⅝in

16.7cm/6½in

21.7cm/8½in

1.5cm/⅝in

END TAB

box side diagram

8.5cm/3⅜in

1.5cm/⅝in

BASE TAB

BASE TAB

1.5cm/⅝in

1.5cm/⅝in

1.5cm/⅝in

1.5cm/⅝in

1.5cm/⅝in

paper sculpture animals (page 70)

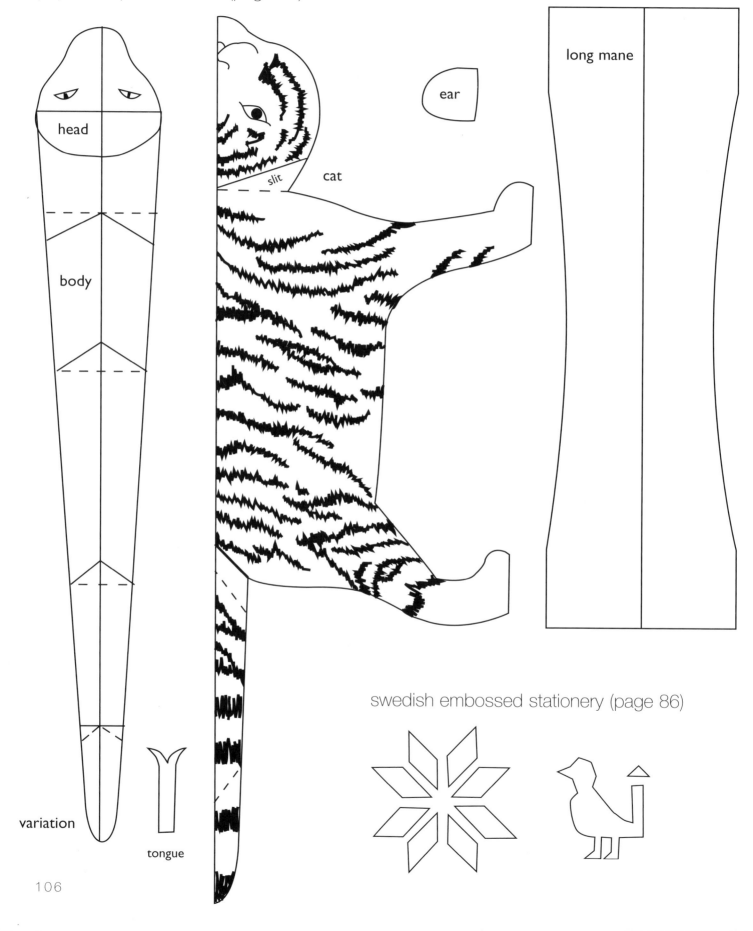

head

body

variation

tongue

slit

cat

ear

long mane

swedish embossed stationery (page 86)

suppliers

 UK

Artbase
88 North Street, Hornchurch
Essex RM11 1SR
tel: 01708 457948
www.artbasehornchurch.com
*shop and mail order for coloured card
and tissue paper*

Calico Pie
15 Queens Drive, Sedburgh
Cumbria LA10 5DP
tel: 015396 21951
www.calicopie.co.uk
*mail order for textured papers,
parchment craft and quilling materials*

Cloud Nine Stamps
The Hideaway
3 Herons Close, Culton Broad
Lowesstoft NB32 3LB
tel: 01502 512583
www. cloudninestamps.co.uk
mail order for stamps, craft accessories

The Craft Depot
Somerton Business Park, Somerton
Somerset TA11 6SB
tel: 01458 274727
www.craftdepot.co.uk
mail order for craft materials

Cranberry Card Co.
37 Cromwell Close, Walcote
Lutterworth
Leicestershire LE17 4JJ
tel: 01443 224442 / 01455 554615
www.cranberrycards.co.uk
*mail order for printed, textured,
metallic and pearlized card and paper*

Crescent Quilling and Papercrafts
4 High Street, Shoreham
Kent TN14 7TD
tel: 01959 525799
www. crescentquilling.co.uk
*shop and mail order for quilling
materials, vellum and mulberry paper*

Dainty Supplies Ltd
Unit 35, Phoenix Road
Crowther Industrial Estate
(District 3)
Washington
Tyne and Wear NE38 0AD
tel: (0191) 416 7886
www.daintysupplies.co.uk
mail order for craft materials

Dark Fibres
17 Blairmore, Rhiconoch by Lairg
Sutherland IV27 4RT
tel: 01971 521 245
www.darkfibres.com
*mail order for handmade papers
including herbs, gold leaf and
field flowers*

Fancy That
New Street Antiques and
　Craft Centre
27 New Street, The Barbican
Plymouth PL1 2NB
tel: 01752 25626
*mail order for rubber stamps,
parchment craft and paper-pricking
accessories*

Fred Aldous
37 Lever Street
Manchester M1 1LW
tel: 08707 517 303
www. fredaldous.co.uk
*shop and mail order for glass
paperweights and craft materials*

Graphicus
Rowantree House, Butterknowle
Bishop Auckland
Co. Durham DL13 5JL
tel: 01388 718770
www.graphicus.co.uk
mail order for printed/coloured papers

Habico Ltd.
Units B4–5, Wellington Road
　Industrial Estate
Leeds LS12 2UA
tel: 0113 244 9810
*mail order for corrugators, deckle-
edged scissors, holepunches, papers*

Homecrafts Direct
PO Box 38
Leicester LE1 9BU
tel: 0845 458 4531
www.homecrafts.co.uk
*mail order for Lazertran paper, glass
paperweights and craft materials*

Jayprint
5 New Cut, Chatham
Kent ME4 6AA
tel: (01634) 813650
www. jayprintcraft.co.uk
*shop and mail order for parchment
craft and quilling materials,
holepunches, origami papers*

Paperchase
213 Tottenham Court Road
London W1P 9AF
tel: 020 7467 6200
shop for handmade papers

Paper Shed
tel: 01347 838253
www. papershed.com
*mail order handmade papers including
silk, banana, sugar cane and metal*

The Papertrail Scrapbook Co Ltd
tel: 01262 601770
www.thepapertrailcompany.com
mail order for vellum, paper and card

 USA

Hygloss Products, Inc
45 Hathaway Street
Wallington, NJ 07057
tel: (973) 458-1745
www. hygloss.com
papers, craft materials

Kate's Paperie
1282 Third Avenue
New York, NY 10021
tel: (212) 396-3670
fax: (212) 941-9560
email: info@katespaperie.com
www.katespaperie.com
decorative papers and stationery

Nashville Wraps
1229 Northgate Business Parkway
Madison, TN 37115
tel: (800) 646-0046
www. nashvillewraps.com
giftwrap, tissue papers

Paper Adventures
tel: (414) 383 0414
www.paperadventures.com
mail order for printed papers

The Paper Source
232 W. Chicago Avenue
Chicago, IL 60610
tel: (312) 337-0798
fax: (312) 337-0741
stationery

Rugg Road Paper
105 Charles Street
Boston, MA 02114
tel: (617) 742-0002
decorative papers and stationery

about the author

Cheryl Owen is a highly versatile and individual craftsperson. She originally trained in the fashion industry, before moving on to apply her flair to mixed-media crafts. Cheryl has since been a prolific and successful craft author and freelance designer for over 15 years, having contributed projects and articles to a number of magazines. This is Cheryl's fifth book for David & Charles, her last two titles being *Making Decorative Boxes* and *Handmade Gift Cards*. Cheryl lives in Highgate, London.

acknowledgments

Special thanks to Cheryl Brown, Jennifer Proverbs and Ali Myer at David & Charles, to Jo Richardson for her attention to detail and to Ginette Chapman for the stunning photography.

index